Lincoln Christian College

P9-CRH-367

Ray W. Pierson
POST OFFICE BOX 1 5 8
PAYSON, ILLINOIS 62360
PHONE (217) 222-5478

preaching
to be
understood

JAMES T. CLELAND

preaching
to be
understood

NEW YORK • NASHVILLE • ABINGDON PRESS

PREACHING TO BE UNDERSTOOD

Copyright © 1965 by Abingdon Press

All rights in this book are reserved.
No part of the book may be reproduced in any
manner whatsoever without written permission of the
publishers except brief quotations embodied in critical articles or reviews. For information address
Abingdon Press, Nashville, Tennessee.

Library of Congress Catalog Card Number: 65-13145

Scripture quotations marked RSV are from the Revised
Standard Version of the Bible, copyrighted 1946 and
1952 by the Division of Christian Education, National Council of Churches, and are used by permission.

251
C625
c. 2

to my wife
in continuing gratitude

58479

preface

The invitation to deliver the Warrack Lectures ("The Preachers Lectureship") is a signal award. I would not dare to claim the unusual position of a prophet with honor in the country of his birth, but I am happy to be remembered in my motherland. Therefore, it is with gratitude that I, a native Scot and an adopted American, acknowledge the invitation from the Committee on Education for the Ministry of the Church of Scotland to be the Warrack Lecturer in 1964.

Many are to be thanked for expediting these lectures. First, there is the Church of Scotland's Committee on Education, especially its convenor. Then there are the authorities of Duke University—the President, the Provost, the Vice-Provost in charge of the Divinity School, the Dean of the Divinity School—who willingly granted me leave of absence from my regular duties. Next, there are my colleagues who both encouraged and disciplined me with their comments. Finally, there are the administrative officers, the teachers, and the students of the theological faculties at the Universities of St. Andrews, Glasgow, Aberdeen, and Edinburgh, who welcomed me to their halls.

Three people deserve mention by name. My secretary, Mrs. Marjean Vernon, wrestled with my manuscript more than once to prepare the final copy, grateful that she would bring to birth but one book of mine! Professor S. K. Heninger, Jr., of the English Department at Duke, helpfully amended my style and, at times, my thought. Miss Harriet V. Leonard, the reference librarian in the Duke Divinity School, proofread the final typescript with a patient, eagle eye.

Some of the ideas in the lectures have been aired before in a bimonthly column, written over six or seven years for *The Chaplain: a Journal for Protestant Chaplains,* published by the General Commission on Chaplains and Armed Forces Personnel. I thank its editor for granting me the right to make use of them as I desired. I am also indebted to various publishers for permission to quote from their volumes, which have been referred to in the footnotes.

Having delivered the Warrack Lectures, I am almost ready to say a *nunc dimittis.*

JAMES T. CLELAND

contents

a point of reference

On November 22, 1963, John Fitzgerald Kennedy, President of the United States of America, was assassinated in Dallas, Texas. A month later there crossed my desk "The Service of Worship" prepared for November 24 by the staff of the Myers Park Baptist Church of Charlotte, North Carolina, one of the most satisfactory churches in America. Liturgically the service was seemly and decorous; homiletically the sermon was right, because it dealt with "a proper sorrow and a proper commitment and a proper hope." The great congregation was steadied and directed. In the course of the sermon, the minister, the Rev. Carlyle Marney, said: "The sorrow is not the sorrow of a century ago. It is a new sorrow. We do not sorrow as men did who were deranged by four years of war. We do not sorrow with the madness that marked the sorrow attending Mr. Lincoln's death." That last sentence pulled me up with a jerk.

At the suggestion of one of my colleagues, I had been reading extracts from the sermons preached in America following the murder of Abraham Lincoln on Good Friday, April 14, 1865. There were four separate and different emphases in these sermons. The first was revenge. Here is a quotation from one sermon preached in Boston by the Rev. E. B. Webb:

Because of a driveling, morbid, perverted sense of justice, the enemy of the government has been permitted to go at large, under the shadow of the Capitol, all through the war. God only knows how much we have suffered for the lack of justice. And now to restore these leaders seems like moral insanity. Better than this, give us back the stern, inflexible indignation of the old Puritan, and the *lex talionis* of the Hebrew lawgiver. Our consciences are debauched, our instincts confounded, our laws set aside, by this endorsement of a blind, passionate philanthropy.[1]

The second emphasis in 1865 was that of the danger of hero worship. These words were spoken in a Baptist pulpit in Hartford, Connecticut, by the Rev. C. B. Crane:

Although we are not aware of it, we have been, for a considerable time past, placing our confidence in our lamented

[1] Lloyd Lewis, *Myths After Lincoln* (New York: Grosset's Universal Library [1929]), pp. 73-74.

President rather than in our God. . . . The destiny of our country was not suspended upon the life of Abraham Lincoln. God has smitten him down upon whom our faith was impiously reposed, in order that He might transfer our faith to Himself.[2]

That thought was echoed in other churches of other denominations.

The third emphasis was of a different order. Lincoln had been slain on Good Friday. Listen to what one preacher made of that fact:

The Rev. Dr. John Chase Lord told his churchmen of Buffalo that no such crime as this had taken place in a thousand years, "perhaps not since the day of the murder on Calvary, when the heavens darkened, and the earth staggered, and the dead rose as the God-Man mediator hung upon the cross. Abraham Lincoln's death by murder canonizes his life. His words, his messages, his proclamations are now the American Evangel. God has permitted him to die a martyr because He wished to consecrate the works, the policy and proclamations of our President as the political gospel of our country, sealed in blood." [3]

The similarity between Jesus and Lincoln was overstressed; martyrdom and Good Friday were again conjoined.

The fourth emphasis, one almost of reverent agnosticism, was spoken at the service in the White House by Dr. Gurley, the Presbyterian minister under whom Lincoln sat when he worshiped in public:

[2] *Ibid.*, p. 82.
[3] *Ibid.*, p. 96.

Gurley, who had known the dead man well, spoke in a simple trust that made plain to them all why Lincoln had liked him. Unlike his class, this preacher saw no reason for this "mysterious and most afflicting visitation" but would wait, serene in the faith that somehow, sometime, God would explain.[4]

Revenge, the sin of hero worship, the Good-Friday martyr, a gentle agnosticism—which was the proper note to be sounded from the pulpit following on a national tragedy? Which minister was "a workman that needeth not to be ashamed, rightly dividing the word of truth" (II Tim. 2:15)? Do you sense the problem? What is the Word of God on such an occasion? On any occasion? What is the gospel, the good news? What is the norm by which a minister judges what he, under God, preaches? What is his point of reference, the polestar by which he steers himself and his folk? Were all four emphases in the Lincoln sermons valid interpretations of the Word of God? Why? Why not? Where does a minister turn so as to find what God says for the contemporary scene? A minister is told that he is a servant of the Word—but which Word, what Word? By what measure does he mete?

I

For those of us brought up in the Reformed tradition the matter of a point of reference is confidently answered: The Bible is the Word of God. How are the lessons intro-

[4] *Ibid.*, p. 112.

duced to the congregation? "Let us hear the Word of God." How are the lessons concluded? "The Lord bless unto us the reading of his holy Word." Some American ministers modify the second sentence: "The Lord bless unto us the reading *and the hearing* of his holy Word." Such liturgical formulae reveal the historic Reformed emphasis. One church historian underscores the emphasis thus:

In the Reformation the phrase "The Word of God" was mighty and prevailed. It was pronounced with assurance and heard with acceptance. To use it was to invoke in one's behalf a divine utterance of incontestible authority, that was documented of old in the canonical scriptures but now freshly reverenced and understood after long centuries of disregard. The Reformation was, or at any rate aimed to be, a reform of the visible church by applying to it the superior authority of the Word of God, so that the Word may be said to be the panoply of the Reformation, its all-sufficient armor and resource. This appears from Luther's early writings through Calvin's whole work, and that of Protestant writers to a much later era, and is a familiar note in our day. . . .

"*Verbum supra ecclesiam.*" "*Ecclesia nata est ex Dei verbo.*" In these phrases the Reformers affirmed the priority and superiority of the Word of God to the visible Church, and in effect made the Word the reforming censor of all that was claimed and practiced in the Church.[5]

Does this mean that *any* scriptural passage is the Word of God? What about the contradictions in the two stories of

[5] John T. McNeill, "The Significance of the Word of God for Calvin," *Church History,* XXVIII (1959), 131.

the creation (Gen. 1 and 2), or in the two narratives of the flood (Gen. 7 and 8)? What does one do with the difference in the purchase price for the threshing floor of Araunah: "Seven pounds," according to Moffatt, in II Sam. 24:24, but "a thousand golden guineas" in I Chr. 21:25? Nahum and Jonah are at odds on God's attitude to Nineveh. Or, from another angle, how does one preach on Deut. 14:21 as the Word of God? "Ye shall not eat of anything that dieth of itself: thou shalt give it unto the stranger that is in thy gates, that he may eat it; or thou mayest sell it unto an alien: for thou art an holy people unto the Lord thy God." If such a transaction is no sin, it certainly is a crime according to the Pure Food and Drug Act in America.

An amendment is obviously in order and is speedily made: The Bible is not the Word of God, but the Bible *contains* the Word of God. This is no new modification. In Calvin's Geneva Catechism of 1545, it is stated that God has left us his sacred Word. Then follows the question: "Where must we seek this Word?" The answer is: "In the Holy Scriptures in which it is contained." John T. McNeill, who was quoted above, comments on this question and answer: "There is a distinction between the statement that Scripture is God's Word, and this one, that God's Word is contained in the Scriptures. God's Word and the Bible are not convertible terms in Calvin's thinking, even though in many contexts attention is not called to the distinction." [6] He goes on to point out that "Calvin of course de-

[6] *Ibid.*, p. 133.

clares for the received canonical books, but like every other discerning reader he has favorites among them. . . . So, while he broadly takes the canonical Scriptures as containing the divine revelation, practically, like all preachers, he has a canon within the canon." [7]

But what is the norm by which we decide *a* canon within *the* canon? On what grounds does one choose *this* passage rather than *that* passage as the Word of God? Here is a quotation from a volume in the Warrack lecture series, one which made me think of Scots congregations singing the 124th Psalm (second version) to Old 124th after the miracle at Dunkirk:

In March 1918, when the German forces breached the Western Front and swept through resistlessly on their way to Paris, consternation reigned in this country. It was a Saturday on which this event occurred and late that night I realized that the message I had carefully prepared was useless. Casting round in my mind for something relevant to the new situation I hit on that thrilling imaginary picture in Isaiah X of the victorious march of the Assyrian king on Jerusalem. "He is come upon Ai; marcheth through Migron: At Michmash musters his baggage; They have passed through the Pass; 'Let Geba be our bivouac.' " At the moment of his triumph when he brandishes his hand over Jerusalem Isaiah beholds him struck down like the fall of the cedars of Lebanon. It was a perfect parallel not only from the military angle but from a spiritual point of view. Isaiah's confidence in the invulnerability of Jerusalem rested on the righteousness of his cause. So one

[7] *Ibid.,* pp. 134-35.

could confidently draw the conclusion that this initial success
of the enemy would in the end prove abortive.[8]

I am sure that the congregation went home strengthened.
But a question haunts me: Why did the preacher choose
Isaiah who said Jerusalem *would not* fall rather than Jeremiah who said Jerusalem *had to* fall? A theocratic patriotism
is one answer. But is this the norm for Christian preaching
in a democracy? What is the Word of God? How do we
find it? How do we recognize it? It is within the Bible, but
where?

Some of us know where the answer is to be found: Jesus
the Christ is the Word of God, the Word become flesh.
This is the theme of the Fourth Gospel. The doctrine of
the Incarnation, the enfleshment, has made the Word of
God visible; it has turned our ears into eyes. Luther was
aware of that: "You ask, 'What then is this Word of God,
and how shall it be used, since there are so many words of
God?' I answer, the Apostle explains that in Romans I. The
Word is the Gospel of God concerning His Son, who was
made flesh, suffered, rose from the dead, and was glorified
through the Spirit who sanctifies." [9] For Luther, Scripture
was "the manger in which Christ lies." The Bible houses
the Christ.

This is the affirmed answer of orthodoxy, Roman Catholic and Protestant. It is interesting to note that it is also

[8] Robert Menzies, *Preaching and Pastoral Evangelism* (Edinburgh,
The Saint Andrew Press, n. d.), pp. 149-150.

[9] Martin Luther, *Three Treatises* (Philadelphia: The Muhlenberg
Press, 1943), p. 254.

the assurance of liberalism, so underrated, if not despised, in our day. President Emeritus Henry Pitney Van Dusen of Union Theological Seminary is emphatic on this point. In a chapter entitled "The Decisive Issue" he uses as a subtitle "The Centrality and Authority of Jesus Christ" and spends 56 pages establishing this fact for liberalism. In an earlier chapter, he wrote these words:

At the heart of Evangelical Liberalism stands Jesus Christ. With some, this central place is taken by the man, Jesus of Nazareth, "the Historical Jesus" or *"the Jesus of History,"* reclaimed by the historical studies of recent years, and now gladly affirmed as both the source and the norm of true Christian Faith. For others, it has been *"the living Christ,"* an intimate Presence within one's own soul (an almost unknown reality for the present generation, one suspects, a phrase without meaning, certainly lacking "existential" reality). But, for normative Evangelical Liberals, *the Jesus of History* and *the Living Christ* are a single organic, indissoluble personal reality. That reality is defined in the life, words, deeds, mind, spirit, faith of *Jesus of Nazareth;* it is known in present power in the *Living Christ.*

The main point is: Liberal Theology in every one of its authentic expressions has been *through and through Christocentric.* More than that; it has been the most determinedly Christocentric theology in Christian history. Indeed, the contention may be advanced that Evangelical Liberalism is the *first* thoroughly and consistently Christocentric theology *in the authentic meaning of that term,* i.e., understanding of God, of man, of human destiny; taking with utter seriousness the central

Christian conviction—that God was definitively present in Jesus of Nazareth.[10]

Donald Baillie was in sympathy with this viewpoint.[11] The quest of the Jesus of history is and will be a recurring question and problem and solution. Therefore, there is an essential duty laid upon us to read, study, and inwardly digest the gospels until we know and have the mind of the Christ.

This second answer as to the content of the Word of God immediately raises problems for preaching from the Old Testament. Shall we become modern Marcionites and reject the Old Testament entirely, concentrating on the New Testament and primarily on the Gospels? What will our attitude be to The First Lesson? A Dutch scholar, Th. C. Vriezen, has put our dilemma in succinct form:

On the one hand there are the attempts of W. Vischer who wants the exegesis of the Old Testament to be dominated by the New Testament, and of A. A. van Ruler, who thinks the preaching of Old Testament and New Testament identical to such an extent that in his opinion the New Testament is merely the explanatory glossary at the back of the Old Testament; the latter surpasses the former in its witness of the Kingdom of God. On the other hand there are the words of Von Harnack, that it is a sign of religious paralysis that the Old Testament is still allowed canonical authority in the Protestant Christian

[10] *The Vindication of Liberal Theology* (New York: Charles Scribner's Sons, 1963), p. 41.

[11] *God Was in Christ* (New York: Charles Scribner's Sons, 1948), Chap. 11.

Church of these days. These conflicting opinions give us some idea of the great tension which, it is true, may have decreased in some measure during the last few years, but is, nevertheless, still latent.[12]

Vriezen goes on to suggest four possible ways of indicating the relation of the Old Testament to the New Testament:

a. typology, which does not only presuppose an organic connection but also *parallelism* between the ideas and the words, though these need not match exactly.

b. preparation, there is an organic connection but the Old Testament idea is present only in part or *in nuce,* and becomes explicit in the New Testament; the New Testament *is in a continuous line with* the Old Testament.

c. similarity, there are religious conceptions which completely correspond or in which the New Testament is entirely dependent on the Old Testament;

d. contrast, there are religious conceptions in the New Testament that form a contrast with Old Testament conceptions.

Only by this differentiation is it possible to express the historical and the organic connection without straining the texts.[13]

There is here the tantalizing problem of continuity and discontinuity between the two Testaments, and these are

[12] Th. C. Vriezen: *An Outline of Old Testament Theology* (Oxford: Basil Blackwell, 1958), pp. 97-98. Used by permission.
[13] *Ibid.,* p. 111.

focused in the teaching and work of Jesus of Nazareth.[14] Shall we test the earlier covenant by the later covenant? Shall we find the activity of the Word, later to become flesh in Jesus, in the pre-Christian testament? If God is the same—yesterday, today, and forever—then is the Word of God, the canon within the canon, the same from Genesis to Revelation? Is there grace in the Old Testament, and justification by faith? Does the New Covenant fulfill the Old? What does one do with "It has been said . . . , but I say unto you"? Does one Christianize the law by finding its completion in Jesus, as one Christianizes the psalms by singing the Gloria after reading them? Shall we lay the emphasis on similarity, on contrast, on both?

It may rightly be pointed out that even for the liberal, the norm for the Word of God was not merely the life, death, and resurrection of Jesus of Nazareth. Van Dusen never limited his Christology in this fashion. Even in the reference cited above he talks as much about *the living Christ* as he does *the Jesus of History*. We must make a place for the doctrine of the Holy Spirit when we seek to find the authentic, authoritative Word. There has been a resurgence in our time of a study of this doctrine, and rightly so.

Its importance is suggested in the title of another of Van Dusen's books: *Spirit, Son and Father*, with the sub-

[14] See Herbert H. Farmer, "The Bible: Its Significance and Authority," *The Interpreter's Bible* (Nashville: Abingdon Press, 1952), I, 3-31.

title: *Christian Faith in the Light of the Holy Spirit.*[15]
Spirit, Son and Father is an unusual inversion of the normal
order, one worth a second thought. There is not time here to
discuss the doctrine, but it is important for us to note that
the Spirit of God and the person of Jesus the Christ are
brought into an inseparable connection. St. Paul uses both
with an enthusiastic abandon in the same paragraph:

But you are not in the flesh, you are in *the Spirit,* if *the
Spirit of God* really dwells in you. Any one who does not have
the Spirit of Christ does not belong to him. But if *Christ* is in
you, although your bodies are dead because of sin, your spirits
are alive because of righteousness. If *the Spirit of him who
raised Jesus from the dead* dwells in you, he who raised Christ
Jesus from the dead will give life to your mortal bodies also
through *his Spirit* which dwells in you (Rom. 8:9-11, RSV.
Italics mine).

To a biblical theologian this may be a doctrinal thicket to
be hacked through, but to a Pharisee converted to Christianity it was—to change the metaphor—all clear sailing.
The Spirit, the Spirit of God, the Spirit of Christ, Christ,
the Spirit of him who raised Jesus from the dead are
synonymous terms. Almost any Quaker would say, "Amen."

Ten centuries later the controversy over the *filioque*
clause recognized the ultimate connection between the
Word made flesh and the indwelling Spirit. The double
procession of the Spirit from the Father and from the Son

[15] (New York: Charles Scribner's Sons, 1958.)

may be a metaphysical conundrum, but the linking of the Spirit with the Son is spiritually satisfying, even necessary. George S. Hendry points out that the addition of the *filioque* clause to the creed of the Western church was "a fruit of Christian devotion." He writes:

It is significant that the interpolation was (in all probability) first made in the liturgical use of the Creed; it was not the product of theological deliberation—indeed, the responsible theological organ of the Church resisted the interpolation for centuries. Here *lex orandi* was *lex credendi.*[16]

It was seen that there must be a norm to test the presence and activity of the Holy Spirit and to define the specific content of Christian thought and action. The testing norm was the mind of Christ known in Jesus Christ the Son and constantly measured by the gospel portrayals.

But the word of Scripture, tested by the indwelling Christ, is not the only norm for the churches in the Reformed heritage. Such a standard is an open sesame to an individualistic, atomistic interpretation of the Word of God. There is surely a place for ecclesiastical, denominational interpretation and definition of the Word revealed in Holy Scripture and tested by the living Spirit of the Christ which became flesh in Jesus. So we come to the controversial and exciting matter of tradition, which is today a key word in all ecumenical consideration.

[16] *The Holy Spirit in Christian Theology* (Philadelphia: The Westminster Press, 1956), p. 40.

St. Paul uses the word "tradition" in a good sense. He writes: "So then, brethren, stand firm and hold to the traditions which you were taught by us, either by word of mouth or by letter" (II Thess. 2:15, RSV). The author of II Peter appealed to his "beloved brother Paul" as one worthy to be listened to (3:15, RSV). Tradition is inevitable if the corporate faith of the church is to have any continuing content. So the united church, through its councils and its bishops, defined the substance of the holy, catholic faith. Tradition was the officially promulgated and universally accepted interpretation of doctrine for all true believers. The Reformation reacted in theory against tradition; *sola Scriptura* was its slogan. Yet the reformed churches produced, in fact, their own traditions in confessions and catechisms and articles. It was inevitable; for tradition is the art of passing on the gospel.

If one has an infallible church and a dogmatic conviction that, under God, it determines the meaning of Scripture in the light of tradition, then there is, theoretically, no room for the church to introduce error in its exposition of biblical truth. But, if one belongs to a Protestant denomination, which has a sense of humor, as well as some embarrassment about its historic meanderings, then one has cause to wonder if the tradition is eternally in accord with the mind of Christ.

The fact and problem of tradition are evidenced in the changing historical relation of the Church of Scotland to the Westminster Confession of Faith as its traditional standard. Until 1905 the ministers of the Church of Scot-

25

land were obliged by law to accept the Westminster Confession in its entirety. It took five years for the General Assembly to approve a new formula, which allowed the ministers to retain the Confession but granted leeway in their interpretation of it. John White put the matter in these words:

Very few today accept the doctrinal definitions as contained in the Confession. On the other hand, very few will deny the *fundamental* doctrines which it sets forth.

No doctrinal statement is final and exhaustive. It is only an approximate expression of truth. It is said that a great change has taken place in the intellectual outlook of men. The social mind or consciousness has assumed a new viewpoint. As a consequence, a new and richer statement of religious truth, relevant to present-day thought and life, is essential. The argument appeals; but is there any agreement amongst our leading thinkers—scientists, theologians, philosophers—as to what this new intellectual outlook is, or any concurrence in defining the new viewpoint which the social consciousness has assumed? [17]

The new formula was as follows:

I hereby subscribe the Confession of Faith, declaring that I accept it as the Confession of this Church, and that I believe the fundamental doctrines of the Christian Faith therein.[18]

[17] Augustus Muir, *John White* (London: Hodder and Stoughton, 1958), pp. 127-8.
[18] *Ibid.*, p. 128.

This now means that the Westminster Confession of Faith is a subordinate standard of the Church of Scotland, its principal subordinate standard. Subordinate to what? To "the Word of God which is contained in the Scriptures of the Old and New Testaments [which] is its supreme rule of faith and life." What does this mean in practice? The Word of God for a member of the Church of Scotland is a majority vote of the General Assembly interpreting a passage of Scripture under the guidance of the Holy Spirit! [19] That majority vote may change from decade to decade, if not from year to year. Yet it is very important for any church to have a corporate decision on the content of the Word at any given time. It may well be that the various Presbyterian kirks should revise the Westminster Confession and the two Catechisms, as they have the *Directory for Worship* and the *Form of Government*.

The need for tradition is always with us; but the tradition should be a lively interpretation of the Word rather than the dead hand of the past. Tradition is necessary. But it is true only when it is the church's best corporate thinking under the guidance of the eternal Spirit seriously considering God's Word for us today.

II

It must be obvious that we have not come to the heart of the matter yet. We cherish the Bible; we acknowledge the

[19] One hearer suggested an emendation to this interpretation. He would add the following words at the end of the sentence: "on the deliverance of an Assembly committee"!

Word become flesh; we are grateful for the Spirit which dwells in the church and in the believer; we accept the corporate tradition. We believe that the Word of God is in each of them. But we still want to know the content of the Word which both Testaments and the Holy Spirit and the tradition acknowledge and proclaim, usually with unanimity, sometimes with variation. When the mediums of the Word speak with varying voices, then there is a moment of crisis in the church. To acknowledge a serious conflict in the interpretations of the Word, one has but to think of the excommunication of the Reverend John McLeod Campbell of the Parish of Rhu in 1831 and his subsequent vindication. The question of the ordination of women to the ministry is a matter for debate and action not only in Scotland but throughout Christendom. The problem is one of an accepted norm, a norm which is found in Scripture and in the Word become flesh and in the tradition, but which sits in judgment, through the activity of the Holy Spirit, upon both Testaments and upon the decisions of the church made in solemn assembly.

Is there such a norm? Is there any unambiguous, central, recurring fact upon which the Bible and Jesus and the Holy Spirit and the tradition fundamentally agree? Surely there is. Is it not something like this: God of his own free will is constantly seeking to bring man into right relations with him, not because of any merit on man's part, but because of God's own nature? He created man for himself and, despite man's blundering and "cussedness" and sin, God makes recurring efforts to bridge the gulf which man has made between himself and God. God is, therefore, not only creator and sustainer—he is redeemer.

This is the refrain of the Old Testament. It is symbolized in the Passover, annually recalled, as the deliverance of the whole nation from bondage. It is recalled in the Prophets: "When Israel was a child, then I loved him, and called my son out of Egypt" (Hos. 11:1). It is recognized as a recurring fact by Second Isaiah: "Comfort ye, comfort ye my people, saith your God. Speak ye comfortably to Jerusalem, and cry unto her, that her warfare is accomplished, that her iniquity is pardoned" (40:1-2). It is individualized and personalized by the psalmists; we still sing their glad songs:

> I waited for the Lord my God,
>   And patiently did bear;
> At length to me he did incline
>   My voice and cry to hear.
> He took me from a fearful pit,
>   And from the miry clay,
> And on a rock he set my feet,
>   Establishing my way
>   (*Scottish Psalter*, 40:1-2).

The Old Testament reveals the fact of a reconciling God.

This, too, is the chorus of the New Testament. "God so loved the world, that he gave his only begotten Son, that whosoever believeth in him should not perish, but have everlasting life. For God sent not his Son into the world to condemn the world; but that the world through him might be saved" (John 3:16-17). "But God commendeth his love towards us, in that, while we were yet sinners, Christ died for us" (Rom. 5:8). The New Testament continues and develops and particularizes the theme of deliverance.

This is also the sum and substance of the brittle, and almost frozen, doctrines of the atonement in the church as contradictorily enunciated by the Epistle to the Hebrews, Abelard, Anselm, and Aulen. The four theories represented there—the sacrificial, the moral, the juridical, and the dramatic—are probably irreconcilable in approach, in expansion, and in detail. But they all point to the same fact— that *God's Word is God in action on man's behalf*. It is the action of the God who was effectively active in the Old Testament. In the New Testament it was still God who acted; Jesus Christ was his agent. Here is how one New Testament scholar puts it, after he has paid his tribute to the work of Jesus:

Yet, for all that, it remained God who had provided salvation; God who carries out the plan of salvation-history; God toward whom the consummation flows; God from whom the call went forth; God for whom the Church is being built as a temple; God whose rule is the goal of all services of Worship. The Lordship of Jesus took nothing from the power of God, but was only the manifestation of the divine glory.[20]

God made himself known of his own initiative. He was, and is, not reluctant to forgive man's sin and to deliver him

[20] Gerhard Delling, *Worship in the New Testament*, translated by Percy Scott (Philadelphia: The Westminster Press, 1962), pp. 119-20.

from the power of sin. He reigns, he acts, he redeems—for our benefit.

Our job as preachers is not only to establish a canon within the canon but, in P. T. Forsyth's words, to find a gospel within the Scriptures: "Remember that Christ did not come to bring a Bible but to bring a Gospel. The Bible arose afterwards from the Gospel to serve the Gospel. . . . The Gospel was there before the Bible, and it created the Bible, as it creates the true preacher and the true sermon everywhere." [21]

For Forsyth that gospel was centered on the Cross and on the indwelling Christ. It is primarily there. But the gospel is also in the Old Testament. My own theological bias is toward the acceptance of "continuity" between the Testaments, rather than "discontinuity." Abraham, Isaiah, the authors of Ruth and Jonah, and some of the psalmists knew God in redeeming action. The Old Testament, too, reveals the gospel within the Scriptures.

There is a manward side to this norm, summed up in the words "faith," "obedience," and "joy." Man trusts this God; man obeys him by worshiping him and loving one's neighbor; man lives with an enthusiastic exhilaration at the heart. This is his response to the gracious action of God in going out to meet man so as to bind man to God in love. It is summed up in "love God and love your neighbor," the two new commandments of Jesus which fulfill all the Law and the Prophets.

[21] *Positive Preaching and Modern Mind* (Grand Rapids: Wm. B. Eerdmans Publishing Company [1907]), pp. 9-10.

The Word of God is the activity of the living personal Creator, Sustainer, and Redeemer made known in the Bible, in the Spirit, and in the tradition of the church. This is a valid point of reference for preaching.

III

John Buchan, Lord Tweedsmuir, in his autobiography tells of a friend visiting wounded soldiers back from Mesopotamia in the first World War. He asked one Scot where he was wounded. He replied: "It was twa miles on the Rothiemurchus side o' Baghdad." John Buchan adds: "His native parish under the knees of the Cairngorms was the point from which he adjusted himself in a fantastic world, and the city of the Caliphs was only an adjunct. Such a race could never be rootless or homeless." [22]

What has been attempted here is an effort to find a homiletical point of reference, a Rothiemurchus, in our spiritual heritage, so that we may be at home as we live and preach in a fantastic world.

[22] John Buchan: *Memory Hold-the-Door* (Toronto: The Musson Book Company, Ltd., 1940), p. 169.

bifocal preaching

Catherine Drinker Bowen in her recent volume, *Francis Bacon: The Temper of a Man,* adds an "Author's Note" at the end of her book. She says, referring to a previous volume which she has written:

Readers of *The Lion and the Throne* have met in this present volume the dramatis personae a second time, I hope with deeper understanding. . . . Occasionally I found it expedient to repeat a bit of historical dialogue or correspondence from book to book, even a descriptive phrase or two of my own where it seemed pertinent; surely an author may plagiarize her own work.[1]

[1] (Boston: Little, Brown & Company, 1963), p. 235.

In line with her assumption that an author may plagiarize her (or his) own work, let me quote some words, which I wrote a few years ago, regarding the Word of God, our homiletical point of reference:

Here is how a group of Duke students and their teacher put that fact after debate and with numerous emendations:

> God, the Creator the Sustainer of life, has so pur-
> posed in His love that man be in right relations with
> Him, that of His own free will He overcomes the
> power and erases the guilt of sin which separates man
> from God. This was always His effective purpose, but
> it was uniquely manifested and dramatized in the
> birth, life, death and resurrection of Jesus. He is
> acknowledged as the Son of God because he supremely
> reveals the will and nature of God. This redeeming
> activity of God is perpetuated by the working of the
> Holy Spirit. Those who believe this are bound in an
> eternal fellowship whose daily life on earth is marked
> by faith, love and hope. Those who refuse to believe
> this are under the judgment of God's love, here and
> hereafter.[2]

The one sentence which caused the class trouble was the last one. Originally the formulation had ended: "Those who believe this are bound in an eternal fellowship whose daily life on earth is marked by faith, love and hope." But the students wanted something said about those who did not believe. There was the quandary. The class was split

[2] James T. Cleland, *The True and Lively Word* (New York: Charles Scribner's Sons, 1954), pp. 25-26.

between those who had an enthusiastic belief in hell and those who were universalists in their confidence that a Father God would ultimately redeem all men. The dilemma was to find a statement which would reconcile both positions! After hours of discussion, it was decided to leave the matter to God, and the final sentence was unanimously, if grudgingly, accepted: "Those who refuse to believe this are under the judgment of God's love, here and hereafter."

Some words from the paragraph following this creed may well sum up the matter of "A Point of Reference":

That attempt to state the Word of God is not perfect. We have enough of a sense of humor, if not of humility, to refuse to believe that creation has been groaning and travailing for hundreds of years to produce a professor and a class which would say the definitive word on the Word of God. But we believe we are not entirely wrong. . . . The whole Bible reveals the Word of God, which was, and is, and will continue to be.[3]

There are three aspects to the point of reference, which Paul, along with Forsyth, refers to as "the gospel." First, it is *the* gospel: "For I am not ashamed of the gospel of Christ" (Rom. 1:16). It is an objective statement of a body of facts about God and his Christ and the Spirit and the tradition which a believer knows to be valid. Second, it is *our* gospel: "Whereunto he called you by our gospel" (II Thess. 2:14). It is an affirmation of the effective good news of the contemporary church. That means for us a

[3] *Ibid.*, pp. 26-27.

35

knowledge of the creeds of the universal church, of one's denominational heritage, and of the current ecumenical outlook. Third, it is *my* gospel: "In the day when God shall judge the secrets of men by Jesus Christ according to my gospel" (Rom. 2:16). The gospel and our gospel have been taken possession of by the individual, because they have taken possession of him. He knows what he has believed; he believes what he knows. It may differ in emphasis from one person to another, but each may be saved from heresy through his constant testing of *my* gospel by *the* gospel and *our* gospel.

I

Let us look more fully at the preached content of the gospel, the Word of God, and let us do so by coming at it from our own experience. Let us go to two different services of worship, primarily as sermon "tasters." In one the minister is seemingly a biblical preacher. He starts with the Bible; he continues with the Bible; he ends with the Bible. He announces a text; he discusses the text; and he is still with the text when he says, "Amen." When he wishes to emphasize a point, he thumps the pulpit Bible or, in America, he holds aloft in the air a smaller edition of the Scriptures. When he wishes to clinch a point, he quotes a section of Holy Writ by chapter and verse. When the sermon is over, there is one comment which may be made without too much fear of contradiction: "He seems to know his Bible." Why not? He majors in it and minors in it.

In the other service the preacher is obviously aware of the contemporary situations which confront his people: individual and social, national and international. He analyzes the impinging environment with understanding and clarity. He may even suggest current problems which his hearers had never thought about until they listened to him. He is aware of the milieu in which they live, both from his reading and from his pastoral visiting. Sometimes the world is a battleground; sometimes it is a vale of tears; always it is a vigorous reality. The world is very much with him, late and soon, round the clock. He has his feet on the ground, because he walks the ways of men. This preacher knows in which century he lives.

What makes each of these men tick? The first is so rooted and grounded in the Bible that he spends his time going to and fro between heaven and earth, and between 1200 B.C. and A.D. 150. He knows more about Jerusalem than he does about the city in which his parish is located. He is more at home with the twelve apostles than he is with his own kirk session or vestry or board of stewards. He is more aware of the hostility of the Pharisees than he is of the people who live "on the other side of the tracks." He thinks he is a divider of the Word of God. Sometimes he is. More often, however, he is a biblical archaeologist or a very ancient historian. H. E. Fosdick, back in the twenties, described this type of minister:

Many preachers, for example, indulge habitually in what they call expository sermons. They take a passage from Scripture and, proceeding on the assumption that the people attending church that morning are deeply concerned about what the passage means, they spend their half hour or more on historical exposition of the verse or chapter, ending with some appended practical application to the auditors. Could any procedure be more surely predestined to dullness and futility? Who seriously supposes that, as a matter of fact, one in a hundred of the congregation cares, to start with, what Moses, Isaiah, Paul, or John meant in those special verses, or came to church deeply concerned about it? Nobody else who talks to the public so assumes that the vital interests of the people are located in the meaning of words spoken two thousand years ago. The advertisers of any goods, from a five-foot shelf of classic books to the latest life insurance policy, plunge as directly as possible after contemporary wants, felt needs, actual interests and concerns. Even moving picture producers, if they present an ancient tale, like Tristan and Isolde, are likely to begin with a modern girl reading the story. Somehow or other, every other agency dealing with the public recognizes that contact with the actual life of the auditor is the one place to begin. Only the preacher proceeds still upon the idea that folk come to church desperately anxious to discover what happened to the Jebusites. The result is that folk less and less come to church at all.[4]

Now, Fosdick was wrong on two counts: One, more and more people are coming to church in the United States; two, it is possible to be an interesting, perhaps an exciting, expositor of the Bible. Even so, there was, and is, truth in

[4] Harry Emerson Fosdick, "What is the Matter with Preaching?" *Harper's Monthly Magazine*, CLVII (July, 1928), 134-35. Used by permission.

his critical generalization. O. Douglas, in her urban-kailyard novel *The Setons*, has this to say of family worship in a Glasgow manse:

> Elizabeth rose and detached the kitten, taking it and Buff [her small brother] on her knee, while her father opened the Bible and read some verses from Jeremiah—words that Jeremiah the prophet spake unto Baruch the son of Neriah in the fourth year of Jehoiakim, the son of Josiah, king of Judah. Elizabeth stroked Buff's mouse-coloured hair and thought how remote it all sounded. This day would be full of the usual little busy-nesses—getting Buff away to school, ordering the dinner, shopping, writing letters, seeing people—what had all that to do with Baruch, the son of Neriah, who lived in the fourth year of Jehoiakim? [5]

A few pages later, in answer to her father's suggestion that she run away because he was busy, she answers:

> "Yes, I'm going. There's just one thing—about the chapter at prayers. I was wondering—only wondering, you know—if Baruch the son of Neriah had any real bearing on our every-day life?
>
> Mr. Seton looked at his daughter, then remarked as he turned back to his work: "I sometimes think you are a very ignorant creature, Elizabeth." [6]

[5] O. Douglas, *The Setons* (London: Hodder and Stoughton, Ltd., 1917), p. 41.
[6] *Ibid.*, p. 45.

Family worship, rather than preaching, was the cause of that interchange. But those of us who are older remember ministers who spent so much time in the study with their Bibles and concordances and commentaries, and so little time in the parish with their flock, that it could be said of them, with some truth, that they were invisible six days in the week and incomprehensible on the seventh.

The second of our preachers at least begins where Fosdick thought he ought to begin. He starts with the real problems of the contemporary world in which his gathered congregation has to live. He is acutely conscious of the *status quo*, which a Jamaican preacher once described as "Latin for the bloody mess we are now in." He knows the variety of little messes which coagulate and form the all-encompassing bloody mess. He recognizes the symptoms; he is not unaware of the causes; he can point to the outcome. He is a diagnostican *par excellence*. But, too often, he has no saving Word of God which shows his folk how to remedy the illness, or how to live with it, or how to die because of it— yet without fear. He does not comfort his people, in the root sense of "making them strong in a fellowship." Or, if he does offer a saving solution, it is in *general* terms as contrasted with the *detailed specificity* of the analyses: "Trust God," or "Love Jesus," or "Behave like Christians." The congregation becomes more acutely aware of what they dreaded before they came to church. He discomfits them without comforting them. My own mother, in Scotland, once wrote me a short, but acute, criticism of a sermon she had just heard: "The minister led us down into deep water—and left us there." She was not drowned, but she was soaked; and she was as mad as a wet hen. This, too often, is a valid description of much preaching.

Each of these men is guilty of a homiletical heresy, the heresy of "mono-focality." Each is a "circle" preacher, with but one sermonic center. The first preacher is so centered on the Bible that he forgets that his congregation lives in the twentieth century. The second is so taken up with the present scene that he forgets that God, being eternal, has always a Word for the current situation, a Word which may well be found in God's dealings with the past. Each man suffers from the vice of a virtue. The first is vicious, because he neglects the people in front of him. He is so taken up with what God once said that he overlooks what this means when immersed in today's living. This is true even "furth of Scotland." Here is the confession of an Episcopalian Bishop in the United States:

I had prepared a sermon which had been, I doubt not, profitable to me, but which was so utterly ineffective as a sermon that I took the liberty of asking a very discerning friend what was the difficulty with it. His reply was the best criticism I ever received. "You seeemed to me," he said, "to be more concerned about the truth than about men." Yes, that was the difficulty. I saw it in a moment. I had no right as a preacher to be concerned about the truth. I should have had the truth in command, so that I could have given my whole concern to men. As it was, the sermon lacked authority.[7]

[7] William Jewett Tucker, *The Making and the Unmaking of the Preacher* (Boston: Houghton Mifflin and Company, 1898), pp. 20-21.

Notice the Bishop's diagnosis of his homiletical sickness: "the sermon lacked authority" because it was "more concerned about the truth than about men." Our concern is not merely with what was once true in sacred history; our concern is also with the urgent present: What is the Word of God for *and in* this pressing problem, today, just now, specifically if possible? The second of our preachers is also vicious, because he is so taken up with people and their anxieties that he has forgotten that God may have some Word from the past which actually speaks to people in the rough and tumble, in the sickness and pain, of so much of our daily existence. He loves people; he is worried by what upsets them. He carries them in his heart and on his mind —even in his stomach and duodenum until he develops ulcers. It was said, often, of a prominent preacher in Washington, D.C.: "What John preaches about Sunday morning depends on what he gets mad at Saturday night." [8]

The description of each of our two preachers is caricature: an exaggeration of a single characteristic for the sake of emphasis. Yet there is truth here. One is Bible centered; the other, man centered. One spends his time in the Book of God; the other spends his time in the world of man. Each is guilty, homiletically, of the heresy of "mono-focality."

II

Homiletical orthodoxy, within our religious heritage, is that a sermon is not a circle but an ellipse. It does not

[8] W. F. Dunkle, Jr., "Planning a Year's Work," *The Pulpit*, XXXIV (1963), 7.

have a single focus but two focuses. It is not a case of being
Bible centered, or man centered. It is the conscious, careful
recognition of both the historic faith and the folk in front
of the pulpit. There are always two centers of interest in
a sound sermon—the historic faith and the present day.
Which is more important? The answer is: Which focus is
more important in drawing an ellipse? Both are indispensable. Together they form the Word of God.

Our first job is to find a valid designation for each of
the two focuses. One is very simply and accurately labeled
the "Contemporary Situation," with a capital C and S. I
used to call the other the *Weltanschauung,* which is both
highfalutin and inaccurate. Then I tried a translation of
that word: "world view," but my students objected. They
were not enthusiastic about the use of "world," which is
linked for them with "the flesh and the devil." Perhaps
"gospel" is the term. But it is so limited, either to the
teaching and work and person of our Lord or to the writings
of the four evangelists, that it ignores the Old Testament
and, maybe, the tradition. Why don't I use "Word of
God"? I did, until a former assistant pointed out that the
Word of God is constantly, in the biblical records, the
linking of revelation with a Contemporary Situation. The
Word of God is *the* name for the ellipse drawn around
the focuses. That is so basic and exciting a fact that it will
have to be dealt with here in detail. And it will be. But
our immediate problem is a term for that other focus. I
thought of "Credo," but, being a first person singular verb,

it is too subjective in its denotation and connotation. Therefore, it has seemed best to use a translation of gospel:
"Good News," recognizing that this Good News is found
in the Old as well as in the New Testament. A diagram
of this view of homiletical orthodoxy would appear thus:

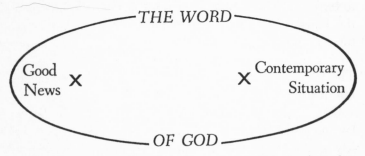

Now let us examine the thesis that a Word of God is
always the Good News (or an aspect of it) immersed in
a Contemporary Situation. Is it not true that our understanding of the content of various Old Testament books
has been clarified with the dating of these books by internal
and external historical events? The prophets were not
foreseers of a distant future; they were men of their own
time who combined their confidence in Yahweh with what
was happening around them. Then they drew spiritual-
political conclusions and "prophesied," for the present and
the *immediate* future. Ruth makes more sense when interpreted in the light of a protest against the attitude of
Ezra and Nehemiah who required the Jews to divorce
foreign wives, than when read *in vacuo*. The literal and
spiritual conclusion of Ruth is that David, the great king,

had Moabite blood in his veins! Jonah is a plea for a wider vision of God's love than postexilic exclusiveness permitted. Nineveh, that wicked city, is on God's heart, as well as Jerusalem, the holy city. Part of Isaiah becomes Second Isaiah because of the specific (even shocking!) reference to Cyrus as the Messiah, who would deliver the Jews from the Babylonian captivity. Is it not valid to deduce, from these and other instances, that "Thus saith the Lord" and an immediate and local situation are particularly joined? The Word of God *is* bifocal. It has its head in the heavens, but its feet are on the ground.

Our Lord worked with both focuses. An ecclesiastical lawyer asked him a question, to which Jesus replied by having the lawyer answer it himself: "Teacher, what shall I do to inherit eternal life?" Jesus asked him: "What is written in the law?" You know the scribe's comeback: Love God and love your neighbor as much as you love yourself. Jesus suggested that the lawyer try it. Do you recall the next exchange: "But he, desiring to justify himself, said to Jesus, 'And who is my neighbor?' " One would imagine that Jesus would be interested in such a query, maybe that he would even suggest group discussion, a round table, a symposium on so vital an issue. But he did not. He told as nasty a parable as a Jew ever listened to. We somewhat sidestep the impact of the story by calling it "The Good Samaritan." For most Jews the Samaritan was a bastard—possibly literally, certainly spiritually. Perhaps homileticians read too much into the ending of the parable when they point out that the lawyer was unwilling, or

unable, to speak the word "Samaritan" when Jesus asked:
"Which of these three, do you think, proved neighbor to
the man who fell among robbers?" He said: "The one who
showed mercy on him" (Luke 10:25-37, RSV). The
Parable of the Samaritan is another example of the Good
News poignantly immersed in a local situation. I think it
was Halford Luccock of Yale University who pointed out
that Jesus was not put to death because he talked about
the lilies of the field, but because he made statements like
"You serpents, you brood of vipers, how are you to escape
being sentenced to hell?" (Matt. 23:33, RSV.) Jesus was
embarrassingly pertinent.

Paul was not far behind his Lord. We may prefer to
preach on Rom. 8:28-39, and I Cor. 13, and Phil. 4:8-9.
But do not let us forget what Paul said about the treatment
of loafers in Thessalonica (II Thess. 3:6-12), and about
the behavior of gluttons at the Lord's Supper in Corinth,
(I Cor. 11:17-22), and about his radical surgery for the
Judaizers in Galatia (Gal. 5:12). "The care of all the
churches" was subject material for Paul's preaching, as well
as for personal contacts in his pastoral counseling. Paul's
Good News was never divorced from the daily walk and
conversation, from the limping walk and acrimonious conversation, of the scattered churches up and down the eastern
end of the Mediterranean.

This bifocal approach is repeated in the church's life and
worship. Think of Francis in Italy, and Calvin in Geneva,
and Knox in Edinburgh, and Chalmers in Glasgow. What
lay behind the social gospel movement in America? What

lies behind the Iona Community in Scotland? Is it not an acute awareness that the Word formerly proclaimed and eternally respoken is a Word for the immediate present? But that Word, in order to be heard and seen and accepted, has to be shown forth in today's garments, speaking to today's needs and worries.

Listen to John Wesley. He is 88 years old. The date is February 23, 1791. The day before he has preached the last of more than 40,000 sermons. He will be dead in less than a week. He is writing a letter to William Wilberforce. What has this old preacher to say to a statesman who is wrestling with the problem of slavery in the political arena? Here is most of the letter:

Dear Sir: Unless the divine Power has raised you up to be as *Athanasius contra mundum,* I do not see how you can go through your glorious enterprise in opposing that execrable villany, which is the scandal of religion, of England, and of human nature. Unless God has raised you up for this very thing, you will be worn out by the opposition of men and of devils. But if God be for you, who can be against you? Are all of them together stronger than God? O be not weary in well doing! Go on in the name of God and in the power of His might, till even American slavery (the vilest that ever saw the sun) shall vanish away before it.

Your affectionate servant.[9]

There are not a few Methodists south of the Mason-Dixon line in the United States who wish that John Wesley

[9] *The Letters of John Wesley,* edited by John Telford (standard edition; London: The Epworth Press, 1931), VIII, 265.

had died a week sooner than he did. Yet he was merely repeating himself. No, he was repeating what he believed to be a Word of God and applying it to his own time. This is bifocal writing and preaching and living.

Every year *Time,* a weekly news magazine in the United States, chooses for its first issue in January the "Man of the Year," for the previous year. The criterion for selection is the "man or woman who dominated the news of that year and left an indelible mark—for good or ill—on history." Sometimes an individual is chosen: Roosevelt, Churchill, Stalin, Queen Elizabeth. Sometimes a group is recognized in a symbolic figure: the Hungarian Freedom Fighter, Korea's G.I. Joe. In 1964 a Negro was chosen for the first time, a Negro worthy of choice for his own indelible mark on current history, and worthy of choice as the representative of his race, which made the headlines throughout 1963. He is a clergyman, the Reverend Martin Luther King, Jr., who is our word "bifocality" become flesh. He is a Baptist, a college and seminary graduate who chose the ministry as "the only framework in which he could properly position his growing ideas on social protest." [10] King himself comments: "From my background I gained my regulating Christian ideals. From Gandhi I learned my operational technique." [11] He preaches *from* the Bible *to* the American scene, as can be gathered from the title of one sermon in a volume which he recently

[10] *Time,* January 3, 1964, p. 14.
[11] *Ibid.*

48

published: "Paul's Letters to American Christians." [12] The style is Pauline; quotations from the canonical epistles are interwoven with King's own imaginary paragraphs. It is almost as moving an epistle as his famous "Letter from a Birmingham Jail," written to a group of white clergymen who had publicly criticized him for "unwise and untimely" demonstrations. Is there a sit-in in Atlanta, Georgia? King is there. Is there a bus boycott in Montgomery, Alabama? King is there. Is there a protest march in Albany, Georgia? King is there and goes to jail. Round him gather the clergy —white and colored; ministers, priests and rabbis—marching to prison in fellowship, with their Bibles tucked under their arms. Even the Stated Clerk of the United Presbyterian Church in the U.S.A. was arrested. King speaks with the powers that be: the President of the United States, governors of the states, mayors of cities. He talks with his own people in any social stratum. John Wesley must wish that King were a Methodist. Our Lord must be glad that he is a Christian, a bifocal Christian.

The Word of God, then, is always the Good News, or an aspect of it, immersed in a Contemporary Situation. A sermon is an ellipse. Bifocality is the hallmark of homiletical orthodoxy.

III

Let us look at each focus separately, remembering that both must needs be conjoined. Where do we turn to find the

[12] *Strength to Love* (New York: Harper & Row, 1963), pp. 127-34.

content of the Good News? It is primarly contained in the Bible, in various parts of all the Bible. From Genesis to Revelation God sought to bring man into such a relationship with God that man would seek to express that relationship by loving God and by loving his neighbor as himself. But it is important for us to notice that the Good News is also found elsewhere. It is expressed in the creeds of the church, in the confessions, in the catechisms, and in the articles of religion. If we wish to preach a series of sermons on the Apostles' Creed, then we might well read Ronald Knox, *The Creed in Slow Motion*.[13] It is a Roman Catholic study, and sometimes our Protestantism will gasp and gag at what is said; but it does reveal how a creed can be preached so that the listener may grasp the content right where he sits. These sermons were originally delivered to teen-age girls in England during the Second World War.

The Good News and man's response to it are also found in the prayers of Christendom. We would be wise, on occasion, to use as one sermonic focus a great prayer from one of the many collections published for our benefit. Massey H. Shepherd, Jr., has written an excellent interpretation of *The Book of Common Prayer* entitled *The Oxford American Prayer Book Commentary*.[14] It is an indispensable volume for both liturgical and homiletical preparation.

Similarly, the hymns of the church are a gold mine for our reflection on the Good News, where theology is penetrated and revivified with piety. Some years ago Albert

[13] (New York: Sheed and Ward, 1949.)
[14] (New York: Oxford University Press, 1950.)

E. Bailey examined the hymns which people love to sing, by a study of the commonly used American hymnals. From that inquiry he wrote an excellent study, in an anecdotal and biographical form, telling of the authors and of the influence of the hymns in the worship and life of the church. The title of the volume tells why it is valid source material for the Good News: *The Gospel in Hymns.*[15] Its subtitle is *Backgrounds and Interpretations.*

Do not forget the lives of the saints, with a capital "S" and a small "s." Read the biographies of old saints and new saints, great saints and second-division saints, those known to the church and those known only to God and, now and again, to you and me. One may well go beyond biography to other forms of literature. Time fails me to tell of Auden and Bunyan, of Dante and T. S. Eliot, of Fry and C. S. Lewis, of Milton and Pascal, of Shakespeare and Shaw, of Tolstoi and others whom you already know and love and use. Professor Charles Osgood, in his Stone Lectures at Princeton Theological Seminary in 1940, said these valid words: "Secular literature cannot equal Holy Writ in power or authority or efficacy as a means of grace. Yet it may illustrate, reinforce, verify, and illuminate Holy Writ. . . . It may serve us as the sycamore tree served Zacchaeus, to gain a clearer sight of the Incarnate Truth." [16] I know that these words are true. Yet, for me, they are not the

[15] (New York: Charles Scribner's Sons, 1950). Cf. Erik Routley, *Hymns and the Faith* (Greenwich: The Seabury Press, 1956).

[16] *Poetry as a Means of Grace* (Princeton: Princeton University Press, 1946), p. 8.

whole truth. It is possible to find a valid "text" containing the Word of God outside Holy Writ. If you do not believe that, then read John Wesley's journal for May 24, 1738, the day of the Aldersgate experience. There is God in action in a local situation. And the world was never quite the same again. The Good News is one indispensable focus.

The second focus is the Contemporary Situation: the people in front of us who hear our sermons. There are certain facts about them which never change, no matter where our parish is located. They are male and female, of all ages. They undergo certain recurring human experiences: birth, childhood, adolescence, adulthood, marriage, parenthood, middle age, old age, death. They are healthy or sick; working or unemployed; good, bad, or indifferent. But there are also certain factors which differentiate one congregation from another. We have to know that, too. They vary in age-grade, in sex distribution, in income sources. They live in the country, in the suburbs, in the city. They are conservative or liberal, religiously and politically.

Have we ever thought of the number of communities in which a faithful church member lives? There are his home and his job, the school to which his children go, and the civic club of which he is a member. There is his town, worried about Sunday movies and comic books on the newsstands. There is his church with its organizations and committees. There is his country, often with internal differences which do not make for peace. There is a world which has become one neighborhood but is not one community.

This focus, too, demands sermonic attention, careful systematic study through days of absorbing reading and hours of pastoral visiting. We may be wisely hesitant to speak on international affairs: What should the United States do about Cuba? What is the Christian position on the European Common Market? How should a Christian behave in the political situation in South Africa? But what impinges on our parishioners should not be alien to us, if the care and cure of souls is our business. We are, most of us, called to serve a parish or a congregation. The burden of a recent Lyman Beecher lecture series at Yale Divinity School—the American counterpart of the Warrack Lectureship—is that "the pastorate does represent the point at which the gospel really engages life." [17] When the Good News really engages life in the pastorate, it becomes a Word of God. When it does not, it does not matter how well we exegete and expound the Good News; it fails to be a Word of God because it has ignored the Contemporary Situation to God's discomfort and man's distress. In 1926 Great Britain went through a political and economic crisis with the "general strike" and the "miners' strike." The former was over in a week, but the miners stayed away from work from May 1 until November 19, when they surrendered unconditionally. Many members of the Church of Scotland depended on the mines for their livelihood, in Ayrshire,

[17] Gene E. Bartlett, *The Audacity of Preaching* (New York: Harper & Row, 1962), p. 12.

Lanarkshire, the Lothians, and Fifeshire. Yet *Life and Work,* the official magazine of the Church of Scotland, only once mentioned the word "coal" during these awful months—and that in a news item on the General Assembly. No one would have known from *Life and Work* of the involved economic and moral issues which sapped the strength of the country. Yet a seven-month strike must have been a crisis issue in numerous parishes. Surely there was some Word of God which embraced both the church's historic faith and such a desperate situation. In my adopted country it has been said over and over again that eleven o'clock on the Lord's Day marks the beginning of the most segregated hour of the week in almost *any* of the fifty states. That is still true despite Martin Luther King, and the Stated Clerk of the United Presbyterian Church, and three of my own Divinity School colleagues who were arrested for picketing a segregated store in January of this year. Then we wonder why the world does not listen to us. Our trumpets give an uncertain sound or no sound, our soldiers prefer camp to battle, and our ranks grow thinner. People look elsewhere for words—for *a* Word to give them confidence and courage for living out their lives in the daily darg.

IV

There are, of course, objections to bifocal preaching. Here are three which are recurrently made and which require comment. The first is that, if we preach the Good News, it is not necessary to be specific about the Contemporary Situation. If a minister faithfully presents the saving power of God, especially through the lordship of Christ and the effective working of the Holy Spirit, then in time his people will live by faith, through love, with hope. There is truth in such a point of view. Yet even Paul found that it did not work. The fruit of the Spirit, that which blossoms naturally from a life rooted in God, ought to be "love, joy, peace, patience, kindness, goodness, faithfulness, gentleness, self-control" (Gal. 5:22-23, RSV). But Paul discovered that these qualities had to be pinpointed in local situations. Read I Corinthians and watch him applying the Good News to schism in the local parish, to the problems of immorality, law suits, marital relations, food offered to idols, disturbances at the Lord's Supper, and the matter of spiritual gifts. It is no automatic matter to apply goodness. Luther, Calvin, Knox, Wesley, Chalmers, Kagawa, Schweitzer, and George Macleod say "Amen."

The second objection is that, even if it is necessary, bifocal preaching is inadvisable. It may cause trouble, because it particularizes. No one is too upset with general principles. It is only when they are applied to daily living that folk begin to shiver and to become angry. "Love your neighbor" is fine; all will accept it. But when one particularizes the neighbor, there is trouble. It is no plea of mine that one should deliberately seek personal inconvenience. Even Jesus crossed the border when he was told that Herod Antipas was inquiring for him. But we should not dodge trouble if it comes in line with Christian duty. Safety has never been a hallmark of genuine Christianity. One may **be** deposed or despised or arrested because he is a Christian. Is this necessarily inadvisable?

A third objection is that, even if it be advisable, it is impossible. It is impossible because, with the best will in the world, we are ignorant of the Contemporary Situation. There is truth here, too. It has been admitted in this lecture with regard to the whole era of international relations. But, as was said before, we are primarily thinking of the parish and its current problems. Here is a doctor who wants to know what the church's attitude is to euthanasia. Here is a lawyer who wants to know how one may live in the realm of grace and in the world of law without becoming spiritually disintegrated. Here is a businessman who is sorely perplexed by the recurring conflict between the Christian ethic and the morality of the business world. Here is a frazzled housewife who has never solved the relationship of justice to mercy in the upbringing of a growing family. Here is a youngster whose loyalties are confused as he tries to live in the two worlds of day school and Sunday school. Problems like these require expert knowledge in specific fields, as well as an awareness of general Christian principles. There are experts to help us right in our parishes, men and women who will be glad to brief us in areas where they are knowledgeable. Moreover, we ourselves may become experts in one area—in prison reform; in the relationship of the minister to the doctor in the care of patients; in premarital counseling which reveals how a Christian marriage is similar to, yet differs from, a civil marriage. We are not sociological pundits; but we may be, we had better be, aware of our congregation's vital, anxious questions in daily living.

The Good News must needs be linked with the Contemporary Situation in its social, as well as in its individual, context. That is both necessary and advisable; it is even possible.

V

Bifocal preaching is doctrinal preaching, because all sound preaching is doctrinal. The primary meaning of *doctrina* is "teaching" and, in Latin, the verb to teach, *docere,* is one which governs two accusatives. It has two inseparable objects: the subject taught and the pupil taught. The preacher is the *doctor* of a *doctrina.* If we think analogically of the doctor of medicine, we are aware that he knows his textbooks, his medical Bible; if he is a good doctor, he also knows his patients. He has mastered the *scientia* of medicine, and he is well acquainted with people. He brings the two together for a healthy, a saving, purpose. As doctors of theology, our objects are also two: the Good News and the people—never one without the other.

Do we grasp what this means? Bifocal preaching is a homiletical corollary of the doctrine of the Incarnation. The prologue to the Fourth Gospel tells us that "the Word became flesh and dwelt among us, full of grace and truth" (John 1:14, RSV). People beheld in Jesus the glory and the grace of God. Because the Word dwells within the

57

preacher, that Word may become the saving words of his sermons. Then each sermon may be a current reincarnation. If it be a real reincarnation, then it treads the common ways of contemporary man, even as Jesus once walked the dusty roads of Palestine.

the homiletical sin of eisegesis

The bifocality of the sermon is a homiletical corollary of the doctrine of the Incarnation. The Word of God is always conveyed in, by, and through a contemporary person or event. Now let us analyze in some detail the necessary steps in so understanding the Good News that we are able to incarnate it once again in a Contemporary Situation, with the result that it becomes for us and for our congregations a *current* Word of God. Let us do so by an examination of two sermonic case studies.

One sermon was preached at an evening service in a

suburban church. The Scripture lesson, from which the text was chosen, was Luke 24:13-35, that lovely story of the first Easter evening, when two disciples walked from Jerusalem to Emmaus and were joined, en route, by the resurrected Jesus. The minister focused his sermon on the second half of verse 28: "And they drew nigh unto the village, whither they went: and he made as though he would have gone further." It was a three-point sermon, inspired by the words "and he made as though he would have gone further." The proposition was that Jesus always makes as though he would go further: first, in social relations; second, in international relations; third, in ecumenical relations. It was obviously an attempt at bifocal preaching. There was a biblical text; there was an awareness of the Contemporary Situation. It was a sermon full of sound Christian doctrine. But it drove me back to the Bible to reread the Lucan passage. I soon found that the minister was not really expounding his chosen text. Because, although Jesus made as though he would go further, he did not. He went in to the Emmaus home and stayed with them for a time. The hymn, "Abide with me," is inspired by the fact that he did abide with them: "for it is toward evening, and the day is far spent" (v. 29). If the preacher had wanted to transpose the actual Emmaus situation to the present day, he should have pointed out that the two men prevented Jesus from going further. Then he might have deduced that, in like manner, we prevent Jesus from going further in social, international, and ecumenical relations. Yet, even that application would not have been entirely honest, because Jesus probably stayed with them of his own free will! The sermon may receive high marks on its knowledge of current events; but one wonders about the explication of the chosen portion of the Good News.

The other case study was a graduation sermon preached to a high school class. It was an exciting, stimulating, enthusiastic address on "Ever Learning," which the congregation was told was a central tenet in the teachings of Paul. The speaker was eloquent about how a graduation was really a commencement. If the students were wise, they would not consider their education completed but would be "ever learning." He sketched some of the areas in which they would be "ever learning": college; nursing school; business training; apprenticeships; the armed forces. He held their attention, because he spoke to them right where they were. But is "ever learning" a central Pauline thought? It occurs in II Tim. 3:7, which immediately raises the question of Pauline authorship. Did Paul pen, or dictate, the Pastoral Epistles? What is the consensus of objective New Testament scholarship? Yet, even if Paul were the author of the Pastorals, does "ever learning" sound like the apostle who was not overenthusiastic about the wisdom of this world? But, supposing one of us still defends Paul's right to advocate "ever learning," notice the context in which the two words are set:

This know also, that in the last days perilous times shall come. For men shall be lovers of their own selves, covetous, boasters, proud, blasphemers, disobedient to parents, unthankful, unholy, without natural affection, trucebreakers, false accusers, incontinent, fierce, despisers of those that are good, traitors, heady, highminded, lovers of pleasures more than lovers of God; having a form of godliness, but denying the power thereof: from such turn away. For of this sort are they which creep into houses, and lead captive silly women laden with sins, led away with divers lusts, ever learning, and never able to come to the knowledge of the truth (II Tim. 3:1-7).

Moffatt translates verse 7: "Always curious to learn and never able to attain the knowledge of the Truth." *The New English Bible* renders it: "Who are always wanting to be taught, but are incapable of reaching a knowledge of the truth." The Revised Standard Version construes it: "Who will listen to anybody and can never arrive at a knowledge of the truth." In claiming Paul as his authority, that speaker was deceiving the graduating class, at least once and probably twice, maybe three times, unless he was addressing a female seminary. He did not expound what was actually said in the verse; even if he had, it is still very doubtful that Paul said it.

In both these case studies the preachers read into scriptural phrases, plucked from their context, what they wanted to talk about. This is the homiletical sin of eisegesis.

I

According to the Greek, eisegeseis is the "leading into" a passage of something that was not originally there. The

third edition of Webster's dictionary defines it more nar-
rowly as "the interpretation of a text (as of the Bible) by
reading into it one's own ideas." The sermon thus engendered may well be Christian in content, a veritable
Word of God; but it is not honestly based on the passage
chosen and announced. The text becomes a magician's hat.
The sermonic rabbit which the preacher pulls from the hat
was not originally in the hat. He found the rabbit in the
hat because he put it there. He can extract the rabbit *from*
the hat in the pulpit because he inserted that particular
rabbit *into* the hat in his study. Most of the congregation
does not know what he has done. That is, in part, why he
can get away with it.

What has transpired is that, somehow or other, he has
managed to lay hold on an idea, sometimes a sound idea,
for a sermon. Then he turns hopefully to the concordance
to find a text which will fit the idea. How do I know? I
have done it myself. In my days as a student assistant, I
wanted to preach a sermon at the beginning of a new year
on "Good Resolutions." But the word "resolution" is not to
be found in the King James Bible. The verb "resolve" does
occur once, in Luke 16:4: "I am resolved what to do." I
welcomed it, and I used it! [1] If you don't know the passage
very well, I can get away with it. If you know the passage,
you will be embarrassed for me, as I should have been for
myself—but wasn't. Why? Because the man who was "re-

[1] It was my thirtieth sermon, preached in Old Kilpatrick Parish
Church on the evening of January 3, 1926.

solved what to do" was the rascally steward who had just been dismissed. In the text he was making up his mind to cheat his master by "cooking" the account books to the advantage of his lord's creditors. Why? So that they might receive the steward into their houses now that he had rightly lost his job. It was hardly *the* text for the first Sunday of a new year, granted the context from which it was invalidly plucked.

Or, it may be, in thumbing through the Bible, that a word jumps out at the desperate preacher who is on the hunt for an idea. On that word he builds a sermon—his sermon, not the text's sermon. A shrewd listener once remarked to me: "If the text had smallpox, the average sermon wouldn't catch it." He had just heard me preach, and I still wonder if his critical shotgun had two barrels.

The homiletical sin which doth so easily beset the preacher is that of eisegesis.

II

When we examine the types of minister who are beset by this sin, we find that they fall into four different categories though, fortunately, there are not many who are notoriously subsumed under all four.

The first is ignorance, sheer ignorance. The preacher is unaware of biblical criticism, lower and higher; of the meaning and function of exegesis; of the content and purpose of scriptural, ecclesiastical, and theological studies. He has been brought up to consider each and every word in the Holy Bible as uniquely and independently sacred. Any word, in its context or out of it, has a saving message for man. Our forefathers used the Bible thus—or are supposed so to have acted. Who are their sons to behave differently? Such a man lays hold on the phrase "It came to pass"; from it he evolves a sermon. It is a regularly occurring phrase in both Testaments. In the concordance which I use the phrase is listed with five references, followed by this note, "This verb occurs many thousands of times"! [2] Numerically it must be one of *the* texts in Scripture. So our preacher writes a sermon on: "The Most Optimistic Text in the Bible." His proposition is that it came to pass; that is, it didn't come to stay. This is our comfort when sorrow, trouble, sickness, adversity afflict us. They will pass; they come, to pass. Or, on Temperance Sunday, he preaches a prohibition sermon on: "Touch not; taste not; handle not" (Col. 2:21), six words taken out of context. What is the context?

Did you not die with Christ and pass beyond reach of the elemental spirits of the world? Then why behave as though you were still living the life of the world? Why let people dictate to you: "Do not handle this, do not taste that, do not touch the other"—all of them things that must perish as soon as they are used? That is to follow merely human injunctions and teaching. True, it has an air of wisdom, with its forced

[2] Robert Young, *Analytical Concordance to the Bible* (Edinburgh: George Adam Young and Company, 7th Edition, n. d.), p. 186.

piety, its self-mortification, and its severity to the body; but it is of no use at all in combating sensuality.[3]

Our preacher expounds as Pauline the opposite of what Paul wrote! Such abuse of the text may be excused in one who is unlearned, though Goethe once remarked that there is nothing more terrible, more frightful (*schrechlicher*), than active ignorance.

A second preacher's approach is marked not by ignorance but by slovenliness, by carelessness in his handling of Scripture, by a slipshod attitude to the Bible. He knows better. But the multifarious busyness of a parish crowds out the time for systematic study. The late Ernest Findlay Scott, the distinguished New Testament scholar, hated telephones, mimeograph machines, and all kinds of bells. He once remarked, with an angry sparkle in his eye: "God hath made man upright; but they have sought out many inventions." That was an exquisite misuse of Eccl. 7:29. But a Scottish minister visiting in America preached on that text, and by "inventions" he meant inventions: the steam engine, machines, electricity, and especially armaments. It was a sermon on the perils of the machine age. The diagnosis was acute and specific; the remedy was very general: "Can we recover, discover, spiritual values which alone can control and direct scientific and mechanical power along worthy lines, and make our many inventions not a curse but a blessing?" This is hardly what Ecclesiastes was

[3] Col. 2:20-23. *The New English Bible, New Testament* (New York: Oxford University Press, London: Cambridge University Press, 1961).

talking about. "Inventions" is not a good translation of the Hebrew noun *hishshebhonoth*. "Many a cunning wile" is Moffatt's rendition. "Many devices" is the Revised Standard Version's translation. Powis Smith suggests "many contrivances." Perhaps "machinations," or the Irish word "shenanigans," comes closer to the Hebrew. Though God made man righteous, he has used his brains for all kinds of trickery, chicanery, rascality. That distinguished preacher should have spent more time with the commentaries and dictionaries. He had had the requisite training.

The third homiletical sinner is marked by plain dishonesty. He occasionally prefers a lie to the truth, because "it preaches better." A student in practice preaching at Duke took as his text, "Though he slay me, yet will I trust in him," the King James Version's translation of Job 13:15. It was a good sermon, but his grade was an F—failure. Why? Because he knew, as he confessed, that this was not the correct translation of the Hebrew. He had read Moffatt: "He may kill me—what else can I expect?" He had read the Revised Standard Version: "Behold he will slay me; I have no hope." He was supposed to have examined *The Interpreter's Bible*, where the exegete is unhappy about the King James rendition, and which the expositor whimsically entitles "An Inspired Mistake?" [4] The student admitted that the verse had been discussed in an Old Testament course and that the professor preferred a translation which suggested the hopeless lot of Job in the face of imminent and nonunderstandable death. The

[4] III, 1004-6.

student preacher, knowing all this, chose the King James translation because it made a better sermon. (He cheered up when he discovered that he could retain the major thought of his sermon if he based it on Dan. 3:16-18, the answer of the three Hebrews to Nebuchadnezzar who was about to deposit them in the fiery furnace.) A congregation has some right to expect truth from its minister as well as inspiration.

A fourth category comprises the many ministers who have a strong leaning toward the allegorical interpretation of Scripture. They are in an ancient, and, presumably, an honorable, tradition: Origen, Augustine, Aquinas, and their Protestant successors. " 'The Bible is one vast allegory, a tremendous sacrament in which every detail is symbolic,' writes Daniélou of Origen's fundamental thesis." [5] The Bible should not be translated only in a literal fashion; it is a spiritual book and its true meaning lies beneath the obvious meaning. Sometimes an objective, historical analysis offers no Word of God, because there is no clue to its meaning for the author or his times. Then the allegorist follows the advice of the Scots layman to a budding preacher: "Ye micht wi' advantage find out a hidden meaning in your text. It will maybe be easier on ye to do that than to find out the real one." [6] So such a minister takes as his text an incident from Paul's shipwreck: "they cast four anchors out of the stern" (Acts 27:29). What

[5] Quoted in Bernard Ramm, *Protestant Biblical Interpretation* (revised edition; Boston: W. A. Wilde Company, 1956), pp. 32-33.
[6] *The Interpreter's Bible*, VI, 1105. Again I am quoting myself!

were, are, the anchors? Memory, vision, prayer, and Jesus Christ. My mother heard that sermon and loved it. Her minister, a most helpful preacher and pastor, was quite committed to the allegorical method. Another of his sermons was based on "Man shall not live by bread alone" (Matt. 4:4). What shall he live by? Admiration, hope, and love.[7] That is true enough. It may be a valid interpretation of what our Lord said: "But by every word that proceedeth out of the mouth of God" (Matt. 4:4), though I have my doubts about "admiration."

The problem with this approach is that it is based on the preacher's ingenuity rather than on his exegetical acumen. Bernard Ramm, a most conservative scholar, has written:

The curse of the allegorical method is that it obscures the true meaning of the Word of God and had it not kept the Gospel truth central it would have become cultic and heretical. In fact, this is exactly what happened when the gnostics allegorized the New Testament. The Bible treated allegorically becomes putty in the hand of the exegete. Different doctrinal systems could emerge within the framework of allegorical hermeneutics and no way would exist to determine which were the true. This was precisely one of the problems in refuting the gnostics. The orthodox wished to allegorize the Old Testament, but not the New. The gnostics accused them of inconsistency. The only method of breaking an exegetical stalemate created by the use of the allegorical method is to return to the sober,

[7] "We Live by Admiration, Hope and Love" is line 763 of Book 4 of "The Excursion" by William Wordsworth.

proper and literal interpretation of the Scriptures. The allegorical method puts a premium on the subjective and the doleful result is the obscuration on the Word of God.[8]

The Very Reverend Sir George MacLeod told of a Scottish minister who compared his congregation to a flock of sheep, himself to the shepherd, and the beadle to the sheepdog, "allegorically speaking," at which point the beadle broke in with the indignant protest: "Allegorical or no allegorical, I consider it a damned piece of impertinence." Allegorical preaching is not necessarily impertinence; it may be true to the Good News. But it is not what it pretends to be: a careful, valid handling of the Word of God as recorded in a passage of the Holy Bible.

Ignorance which may be excused, slovenliness which must be censured, dishonesty which is to be deplored, and allegorizing which is, too often, a fanciful, if not a dishonest, analysis of Scripture are some of the guises of eisegesis.

III

Is there any single word under which these four aspects of the homiletical sin of eisegesis may be subsumed? Is there any single cause for such recurrent vices? It may be dangerous so to simplify the issue, but there is a word which both sums up and denotes the reason. It is "bibliolatry": worship of the Bible, excessive adoration paid to the Scriptures. The adoration takes different, strange, and perverse

[8] *Protestant Biblical Interpretation,* pp. 30-31.

forms, as we have seen. But the nub of the matter is a veneration of the Book, per se. This is exemplified for me in various boyhood memories. I was forbidden to place anything on top of the Bible as it lay on my bedside table. There was trouble brewing if my mother found any other book atop the Bible. If she came across a glass of water sitting on it, then a first-class row was not only brewing but ready to break. Her regular instructions to my brother and sister and me as we left for the morning service were: "Be sure to remember the text." It made no difference to my mother if the minister departed from the announced text with the speed of a rocket. It was biblical preaching if a text were announced. A newspaper man recalls James Moffatt's sermonic openings, "He always began with the same phrase, running it into a single word, 'the-text-of-the-sermon-this-evening [morning]." [9] Knowing that the text often turned up for the first time in the middle of my sermons, my mother pleaded with me: "Begin with a text when you preach in Scotland." Yet, as we have noted, there is no guarantee that the employment of a text will ensure "biblical preaching." [10]

The sight of the Scottish beadle carrying the great Bible into the pulpit is for me a moving experience. I sometimes wish that the congregation stood at such a moment. Maybe it is just as well that it does not. Bibliolatry might become idolatry.

[9] Alexander Gammie, *Preachers I Have Heard* (London: Pickering and Inglis, 1945), p. 91.

[10] Cf. John Knox, *The Integrity of Preaching* (Nashville: Abingdon Press, 1957), particularly Chapters I and II.

IV

What can we do to remedy this eisegetical malady? We must make use of the Bible; it is the primary source of our knowledge of God and of his saving will for man. We are the interpreters of a spiritual heritage transmitted, written down, edited, reedited over a period of 1,400 years. Then the Book was translated, retranslated, paraphrased, and canonized. We are the construers of the Word of God, which we know to be ancient and believe to be contemporary, because it is eternal. It is found in many places, though primarily in the Scriptures.

Therefore, our task is fundamentally one of exposition. "All preaching is expository preaching" was the constant slogan of one of my former assistants in homiletics. We may categorize sermons as "textual" and "topical," "evangelical" and "apologetic," "ethical" and "doctrinal." But behind and beneath all these terms is the fundamental fact of exposition: the understanding of a Word of God in its original and eternal meanings and the immersing of the discovered Good News in a Contemporary Situation. Our approaches to this will vary depending on our hermeneutical stances: literalist, conservative, liberal, neoorthodox, and the like. It will be influenced by our religious environment, by our denominational tradition, and by our personal, spiritual hopes and fears.

But in any event there are three stages through which our reflection must plod before a sermon should be ready for a tentative proposition of its central thought. These are

investigation (or, exegesis) of a historic Word of God,
interpretation (or, exposition) of the eternal Good News
at the heart of it, and application of the eternal Good News
to the Contemporary Situation.

Investigation is the first task: the attempt to find the
Good News at the heart of a Word of God, recorded in the
words of the Bible, or of a creed, or of a hymn, or in the
life of a saint, or in a historical event. In each and every
case this is an effort to find the meaning for *its own time*,
not for ours. This can be done by asking key questions.
Who was the author and had he a right to speak for God?
We may be ready to accept the testimony of Second Isaiah
and Paul, but we may have legitimate doubts about Goliath
and Job's friends. *Where* did he speak? In Jerusalem, or
Athens, or Geneva, and in what kind of situation? *When*
did he proclaim—1200 B.C. or 740 B.C. or A.D. 52 or A.D.
1517 or A.D. 1738 or A.D. 1945? The speaker is always influenced, pro or con, by his historical environment? *Why*
did he speak as he did? What was his personal bias—
legalistic, prophetic, apostolic, or what? *How* did he transmit his message—in prose or poetry, in law or drama, in
parable or letter, in proverb or song? The different genres
require different treatment. Poetry should not be interpreted as prose; parable is a unique form of literary construction with singular rules for elucidation. *What* was he
actually saying, or trying to say, to *his* contemporaries?
What was the gist of his message for *his* own time?

This kind of inquiry demands all sorts of scholarly tools:
linguistic, literary, historical, theological. This is why

courses in preaching should be preceded by studies in Old and New Testament, church history, and systematic theology. The pity is that too often such courses are not drawn upon by student homileticians for sermonic purposes. I suppose most of us hate the term "scribe." It is so easily, though not essentially, identified with "hypocrite." Yet, according to Matt. 13:51, Jesus, speaking to his disciples, said: "Therefore every scribe who has been trained for the kingdom of heaven is like a householder who brings out of his treasure what is new and what is old" (RSV). Commenting on that verse, Sherman E. Johnson writes: "This is Matthew's ideal for the Christian disciple. He should be a rabbi, but one 'trained for the kingdom of heaven.' " [11] As exegetes, investigators, we are scribes of the kingdom. When we have done all this serious study, we should be ready to write a *textual* proposition: a statement, in a sentence or a short paragraph, of the author's confident assertion of the Word of God as it is found in the author's environment, in the setting in which he lived.

Interpretation is the second step: a proving to ourselves for the sake of our congregations that the textual proposition has within it a valid message for all times. Here we lay possessive hands on the unchanging, ever-old, ever-new, divine Good News which is still true when removed from the chronological, geographical, cultural surrounding in which it was originally found. For this stage we must needs know the whole history of the church, especially that

[11] *The Interpreter's Bible,* VII, 422.

aspect which is called systematic theology. We are "the people of the Book." But that Book is the basis for the confessional affirmations which proclaim the faith of the undivided Roman Catholic Church, the Reformation movements, the denominational churches, and the ecumenical church. We are heirs of the tradition as well as of the Bible; God has spoken through both. The tradition is our vital heritage. There we find the faith of the army of God and of our own regiment. Such a study enables us to discover if the textual proposition—the ancient, local, particular Word of God—had a continuing echo and a recurrent message within the ongoing church down the centuries. Was the textual Word reiterated, modified, stifled, denied? There will be some modesty connected with this part of the inquiry, because we are aware that a certain amount of personal bias, due to our ecclesiastical heritage and our hermeneutical preference, will affect our decision. But such a study should result in a refined formulation of the textual proposition which is transformed, in our studied judgment, into an *eternal* proposition: a statement of our ecclesiastical tradition's interpretation of the eternal Good News lying in the text, true for all times and all places.

Application is the third step. If we faithfully investigate and interpret, if we carefully summarize our research in a textual and in an eternal proposition, we shall not have a sermon. We shall have the requisite material for a good lecture, a lecture worth listening to, but only a lecture. One more step is needed before the lecture becomes a sermon: we must apply the eternal truth to a Contemporary Situa-

tion. We have pulled that truth out of its temporary setting;
now we must do the opposite. We have to insert that which
is timeless into time, into our time, into our day and parish.
As Jeremiah spoke to the sixth century B.C. in Palestine
and Babylonia and Egypt, as Jesus addressed himself to
folk in the first century A.D. in Galilee and Judea, so we
speak to twentieth-century man and woman in Scotland and
in the world. Application is the relating of the eternal truth,
discovered by investigation and elucidated by interpretation,
to the environment of the congregation in front of us.
Think of the matter in this way. What is our desire in
preaching? It is not primarily to make people acquainted
with the Bible or with systematic theology or even with
the lives of the saints. Our desire is that, in day-by-day
existence, they may live with God and as God has always
wished and willed them to live. What did we deal with in
investigation (or exegesis) and in interpretation (or exposition)? Was it not some aspect of the Good News recorded
in a local situation which had at its heart an eternal truth?
What do we deal with in application? Is it not the relationship of the eternal Good News to the Contemporary Situation of the congregation, in the church and in the home and
in the world? Both focuses are necessary for a sermon which
is orthodox homiletically. As Jeremiah inserted the Good
News into his day with the fear of Babylonia a constant
threat, as Jesus inserted the Good News into his day with its
problems of Jewish-Roman relations and of Judean-Galilean
hostility, so we must insert the Good News into Scotland
or North Carolina with its fear of atomic destruction,

or growing nationalism, or rampant racism. We have to paint the Good News with local color. We have to let the congregation hear a "Thus *saith* the Lord" and not merely a "Thus *said* the Lord." If we do otherwise we shall be but echoes of the past, rather than voices speaking for the God who is active today and is desirous to be active in us. The eternal Word, discovered by investigation and refined by interpretation, is to become a contemporary Word through conscious application. For without application—usually direct, but sometimes indirect—there is no sermon. It is when a minister sees the Good News penetrating an immediately Contemporary Situation that a Word of God is spoken. Then he is able to write his *final* proposition, which is the eternal proposition once again incarnate in the seething, surging life of his own day.

These three stages in sermonic construction may be remembered by the use of three key words. Investigation, or exegesis, deals with the *then*; interpretation, or exposition, deals with the *always*; application deals with the *now*. And the result? The Word of God is preached.

V

Perhaps a "f'rinstance" is in order. Let us work through these three stages in the preparation of a sermon on the book of Ruth. By investigation we discover the anonymous author lived in Jerusalem probably not earlier than the end of the fifth century B.C. He was perhaps upset by Nehemiah's attempt to annul all marriages with alien women (Neh.

13:23-25) and by Ezra's decree regarding the putting away of foreign wives (Ezra 10:1-18). He made use of an old story to put his point across, the sting of the story coming in the genealogy at the end of the last chapter, where it is revealed that David's great-grandmother was a Moabitess. He showed by means of a family tree that, if Nehemiah's and Ezra's views had been in effect immediately prior to the kingdom, the Jews might not have had the David whom they did get under God. The *textual* proposition is that the judgments of the Jewish officials were not necessarily in accord with the will of God.

Is such a proposition a transitory one or is it eternal? To answer is the task of interpretation. We turn to Jesus' commendation of the despised Samaritan and of the centurion in the Roman army of occupation in Palestine, which must have embarrassed Jewish officialdom. We recall Paul's words about "neither Jew nor Greek, . . . bond nor free, . . . male nor female" (Gal. 3:28) in the church, which was hardly the point of view of the Jerusalem Kirk. We think again of McLeod Campbell, and the official, restricted doctrine of election which he could not accept. So the *eternal* proposition may well be that God's ways are not necessarily those of his worshipers in any day or generation.

There is a third step: the application of this eternal truth to the present. What does it mean for us when we come face to face with the tribal ethic of our day in the nation and in the denomination? God is such a nuisance. He is so apt to disregard the barriers that men, good men, put up. We defeated the Nazi menace stemming from Germany, and Martin Niemöller rose in Germany claiming Christian kinship with us. We smashed the Japanese military threat, and Kagawa of Japan shamed most of us by the consecration of his Christian life. That is so hard a lesson for us to learn. I still recall the personal problem my mother had: to reconcile the historical fact that Jesus was a Jew with the accepted fact that God was a Presbyterian. So our *final* proposition is that God's ways are not necessarily those of his ecclesiastical spokesmen. This message of the book of Ruth, reiterated by Jesus and Paul and McLeod Campbell, says a word to us in the midst of national, racial, and denominational loyalties and enthusiasms—a word which, by the grace of God, we are beginning to hear.

VI

It is in some such way as this that we may avoid the sin of eisegesis: of doing what we will with a text—hopefully to the glory of God—rather than letting a Word of God do what it will, honestly, with us. If we think of the Good News as a diamond, then we have a threefold task before us. First, we chisel the diamond out of the rock in which it was found; that is investigation. Second, we polish the diamond and cut it to reveal all its glory; that is interpretation. Third, we place it in a contemporary setting, as in a ring, for all to see in this day and generation; that is application. This is, analogically speaking, the work of "every scribe who has been trained for the kingdom of heaven."

a bow at a venture?

Having some awareness of what a Word of God is, recognizing its essential bifocal nature, and resolving to avoid the sin of eisegesis, whither do we turn now? There is a Sunday school story which may act as a primer for this lecture. The lesson for the day was I Kings 22, the story of the unsuccessful war which Ahab and Jehoshaphat waged against the king of Syria. Ahab was shot by a stray arrow and died in his chariot. A member of the class was asked to explain the first half of the thirty-fourth verse: "And a certain man drew a bow at a venture, and smote the king of Israel between the joints of his harness." The boy paraphrased, mistakenly but to the point: "A certain man drew

a bow at a venture. He missed the venture and hit Ahab."
That certain man was lucky. It is not often that one misses
a venture and hits a king.

Let us look together at the preacher who draws a homiletical bow at a sermonic venture and not only misses the
venture but also fails to hit Ahab—or Jehoshaphat or
Jezebel, or James or John, or Mary or Martha, or Tom or
Dick or Harry. In so many sermons, the minister aims at
nothing in particular, and hits that nothing right on the
nose. Even when he has a target in mind, it is so vague or
so large that it is hard to pinpoint just at what he is direct-
ing his efforts. Do you remember the enlightening answer
given some years ago to the question: Why do American
golfers defeat British golfers so regularly? The reply was:
"In their approach shots, the British play for the green; the
Americans play for the pin." Do we play for the green or
the pin in our preaching?

Moreover, even if the sermon does aim specifically at
something, it often forgets that the congregation is also supposed to be able to understand and to grasp what that something is. One critic of sermons, himself a good preacher,
has written: "The pedant preacher develops his subject
logically from a point where the people have never been to
another point at which they never arrive, under such cir-
cumstances preaching becomes a pleasant game of sacred
solitaire." [1] That is true of others than "the pedant
preacher." Yet a sermon is supposed to be prepared for the

[1] John Edgar Park, *The Miracle of Preaching* (New York: The
Macmillan Company, 1936), p. 7.

benefit of the people. If it is not to their advantage, why should the minister bother to preach and why should the congregation bother to listen? Is it because of too much "sacred solitaire" that one definition of the verb "to preach" has been "to bore unnecessarily"? Let each of us ask himself the questions: What am I trying to do in a sermon? What, under God, am I expecting to achieve through it?

I

A sermon is part of a service of worship. What is the *raison d'être* of corporate worship? Worship is the act of ascribing to God supreme worth. Worship is "worth-ship." It is the "recognition of the merit of another." [2] There are certain sure marks of Christian worship. It is initiated by God who makes himself known to man. God's prior action is primary. He sought man; he seeks us. He has revealed—and he continues to reveal—his gracious greatness. Such disclosure is responded to with joy. Therefore, "We worship for sheer delight." [3] This is sometimes hard to believe. We may glorify God in our worship; but some worshipers endure him rather than enjoy him.

Moreover, the act is a corporate one; it is the conscious, willing union of believers through common, public worship in a given place set apart to God's glory, at a given

[2] Henry Sloane Coffin, *The Public Worship of God* (Philadelphia: The Westminster Press, 1946), p. 15.
[3] *Ibid.*

time also set apart to God's glory. The corporate sense is not engendered by a mere togetherness. It is clarified by memory of the past; it is inspired by an eschatological hope. At its best it is the conscious union of the visible and invisible church. Dr. Charles A. Coulson, Director of the Mathematics Institute of Oxford University, strikingly illustrated this indivisibility, of the church militant and the church triumphant, in a Communion meditation in the Duke University Chapel.[4] He told of what had happened in a small church in Australia. The minister had been struggling to persuade his congregation to stay after the regular diet of worship for the Holy Communion. His words seemed ineffectual, because only two persons remained. Almost in despair, he wondered if he should cancel the celebration. He decided to carry on. When he came to the Sanctus and said: "Therefore with Angels and Archangels, and with all the company of heaven, we laud and magnify thy glorious Name," the truth burst in upon him. He cried out: "Forgive me, Lord, I did not know I was in such company as that!" Such worship is so exuberantly corporate that it should make us aware of the visible and invisible partners in the public worship of God.

Worship, then, is the corporate offering of praise and self to the God who alone is worthy of unique adoration and complete commitment. Worship is the offering which inevitably flows from understanding appreciation. We sing the "Te Deum laudamus"; we also give ourselves in wit-

[4] Worldwide Communion Sunday, October 6, 1963.

ness and in service. The human response in corporate worship is summed up in the concluding paragraph of the Consecration Prayer which Massey Shepherd has described as an "oblation of the church":

And here we offer and present unto thee, O Lord, ourselves, our souls and bodies, to be a reasonable, holy, and living sacrifice unto thee; . . . And although we be unworthy, through our manifold sins, to offer unto thee any sacrifice; yet we beseech thee to accept this our bounden duty and service.[5]

What is the place of the sermon in such a service of corporate worship? What is its purpose? It, too, supplies a personal encounter with God, as revealed especially in Christ, and propounds the outcome of such an encounter. Two quotations from a good book on worship suggest the content and effect of preaching set in the context of worship:

The mystery of preaching is therefore that through it the everlasting Gospel is contemporized, and not only contemporized but individualized, and not merely individualized but actualized. . . .

The Christian preacher is an instrument by which the Church, the Body of Christ, fulfils its function as "the extension of the Incarnation." [6]

[5] Shepherd, *The Oxford American Prayer Book Commentary*, pp. 81-82.

[6] Raymond Abba, *Principles of Christian Worship* (London: Oxford University Press, 1957), pp. 65, 66-67.

Similarly, Angus Dunn, when he was the Episcopalian Bishop of Washington, D.C., had this to say about the sermon:

Miracles of miracles, the Word of God may come to us through a preacher. A sermon is not primarily a man telling us what he thinks about the state of the world, what he thinks of us or of our duties in life. It is not even primarily his telling us what he thinks about God or Christ or charity or prayer. A sermon is a man's speaking to prepare the way for God's speaking.[7]

Reginald H. Fuller, in an examination of New Testament preaching, has written:

There are three types of ministry of the Word, at least, discernible in the New Testament. There is *kerygma,* missionary preaching to the unconverted. There is *paraklesis,* a renewal and deepening of the apprehension of the *kerygma* in the already converted, and *didache,* the instruction of the new converts and of the already baptized in Christain ethics and doctrine.[8]

It is obvious that our task at the regular diets of corporate worship is not kerygma, in the New Testament sense. C. H. Dodd, like R. H. Fuller, has defined kerygma as

[7] Quoted in Scott Francis Brenner, *The Art of Worship: A Guide in Corporate Worship Techniques* (New York: The Macmillan Company, 1961), p. 35.

[8] *What Is Liturgical Preaching?* (London: SCM Press Ltd., 1957), p. 22.

"the public proclamation of Christianity to the non-Christian world." [9] The majority of our congregation is made up of baptized and communicating believers. They should not be called "the unconverted," if they have confessed Christ with their lips or expect to do so after further instruction in a young communicants' class. The whole service, from prelude to postlude, may be—should be—kerygma to an unbeliever who drops in. But it is hardly *the* word to describe the sermon.

Paraklēsis has a place in corporate worship. It is a recalling of the congregation to the content of the Good News, loved long since, but, perhaps, lost awhile. It is particularly appropriate at an evening service when the saints, the more saintly saints, gather to worship, or on the "high" days of the Christian Year, or at the Lord's Supper.[10] *Paraklēsis* is an attempt to revitalize what was once vital, "hence its object is the confirmation and renewal of the faithful rather than the agitation of the nominal Christian or the conversion of the unbeliever." [11]

C. H. Dodd is unwilling to subsume *didachē* under "preaching." For him New Testament teaching was largely "ethical instruction." [12] Yet it seems good to use *didachē* as one aspect of preaching: the explication of a Word of

[9] *The Apostolic Preaching and Its Developments* (Chicago: Willett, Clark & Company, 1937), p. 2.

[10] See The Epilogue on "The Meditation" in my volume, *Wherefore Art Thou Come? Meditations on the Lord's Supper* (Nashville: Abingdon Press, 1961), pp. 128-43.

[11] *Ibid.*, p. 138.

[12] *The Apostolic Preaching and Its Developments*, pp. 1-3.

God in the joint areas of faith and action, in both the vertical and horizontal dimensions of the Good News, with a view to application in a Contemporary Situation. One defense of such an interpretation would be that the Greek verb *didaskein,* to teach, is used in the preface to the three chapters in Matthew which we call "The *Sermon* on the Mount": "And he opened his mouth, and taught them" (5:2). The early church knew that those brought into its membership by kerygma, and encouraged by *paraklēsis,* had also to be instructed through *didachē. Didachē* may be the primary task of the Sunday school and the Bible class. But, if it be located only in these areas, thousands of worshipers will never be instructed, however much they may be exhorted or reassured.[13] Teaching is necessary if the faithful are going to be able to give reasons for the faith and the hope that is within them. This is no new or strange doctrine. Here are some words from a wise Warrack Lecturer. He is contrasting the biblical acumen of Scottish congregations at the turn of the century with the biblical ignorance of similar congregations fifty years later:

How has this come to pass—and in Scotland of all places, where we have ventured to pride ourselves on the nation-wide reach of a highly educated ministry over a highly educated democracy? It would take a full-scale enquiry to discover all the reasons in all their complexity, but I strongly suspect that

[13] In this discussion of these three Greek nouns I have drawn heavily on an article "Preaching" which I wrote for *The Westminster Dictionary of Christian Education,* edited by Kendig Brubaker Cully (Philadelphia: The Westminster Press, 1963), pp. 512-15.

a central one would be found to be a failure of the pulpit in
my generation to do its full duty by the pew. As regards the
whole matter of biblical criticism we have been too reticent,
too timid, too little trustful of the intelligence of the ordinary
man. We have forgotten that the Church's duty of instruction
to its members, never less important than that of exhortation,
becomes doubly important in an age of cultural upheaval, and
that the pulpit is the keypoint of it.[14]

Paraklēsis and *didachē*, reassurance and teaching, are the
hallmarks of the sermon set in the context of corporate
worship.

II

We need to narrow the purpose of the sermon further if we
hope to combat the purposelessness of so much preaching.
It is necessary to look at ourselves as craftsmen, even as
technicians, in planning the general and particular direction of any single sermon. There are automatic objections to
this consideration of ourselves as "spiritual engineers." But
we are. Bartlett, who has been quoted before, has wise
words on this matter:

Nothing is more deadly than our becoming mere mechanics
or technicians in preaching. But neither can we let failures
of craftsmanship stand in the way of the freshness and renewal
which are gifts of the Spirit. In all honesty, we must confess

[14] A. C. Craig, *Preaching in a Scientific Age* (New York: Charles
Scribner's Sons, 1954), p. 45.

that again and again it is our crudities and undisciplined preparation which stand in the way of real communication in preaching. To be insufficient is one thing; to be careless is quite another. So when we seek a mastery of specific skills it is that the sermon may become an adequate instrument worthy of our claim.[15]

The man who has taught me more than anyone else about defining the purpose of a sermon is a layman, Alan H. Monroe, Professor of Speech at Purdue University in Indiana. His volume *Principles and Types of Speech* ought to be required reading for all preachers.[16] I gladly and publicly acknowledge my debt to him in the ensuing discussion of the "general end" and the "specific intent" of a sermon, even though I do not follow him *in toto*.

The general end of a speech according to Monroe, "denotes a general class of speech purpose in terms of the reaction which the speaker wants from his audience." [17] The content of the speech is, at this point, taken for granted. The immediate job is to relate the content to the listeners with a conscious purpose in mind, first for the minister as speaker, second, for the audience as hearer. Monroe lists five general ends, but we shall ignore one of them so far as the pulpit is concerned. It is "to entertain."

[15] Bartlett, *The Audacity of Preaching*, p. 50.

[16] (4th ed.; Chicago: Scott, Foresman, and Company, 1955). This volume has passed through five editions: 1935, 1939, 1949, 1955, 1962. It is the basic text in speech in many American colleges, universities, and theological schools.

[17] *Ibid.*, p. 168.

There are occasions when our legitimate object will be to have the listeners enjoy themselves: the after-dinner speech, a popular lecture, the presentation of athletic awards. One's job then is to pass a given amount of time pleasantly, without hurt. This is hardly the function of the sermon.

The other four general ends are as valid in the pulpit as on the secular platform. The first is "to stimulate," when we "are trying to inspire, to arouse enthusiasm, or to deepen a feeling of awe, respect, or devotion" on the part of the congregation.[18] This is obviously our purpose in *paraklēsis*. We are making no attempt to change anyone's beliefs; our desire is to confirm the listener in a point of view already accepted. Perhaps a better term than "to stimulate" is "to revitalize"—to make consciously vital what has, formerly and continually, been accepted as vital. The particular purpose is revival, that is, to revive what was once "vived." It is to make patent what is latent. We are not dealing with new emphases or aspects of the faith, but with the perennial themes which have to be called to remembrance. Such a sermon is a persuasive one. But it is an appeal primarily to the heart rather than to the head, intentionally to the emotions rather than to the intellect or to the will. We want our hearers to be stirred inside with shame and appreciation, with sorrow and joy, as they remember some forgotten aspect of the Good News. To revitalize is *the* general end for the meditation at the Holy Communion, and at Christmas and Easter. We want to make all the worshipers consciously glad that they are

[18] *Ibid.*, p. 169.

members of the beloved community which is the church.

Not all our sermons should be subsumed under *paraklēsis*; there is the necessity of teaching. Two general ends implement *didachē*. One is "to explain." The Presbyterian minister is "the teaching and preaching elder," and the two adjectives are not to be separated in the pulpit. We are to speak "the truth in love" (Eph. 4:15). But the truth has to be explained, by a constant hammering away at it. This is repeated New Testament counsel. Here is Phillips' paraphrasing of II Tim. 4:1-5:

I urge you, Timothy, as we live in the sight of God and of Christ Jesus (whose coming in power will judge the living and the dead), to preach the Word of God. Never lose your sense of urgency, in season or out of season. Prove, correct, and encourage, using the utmost patience in your teaching. For the time is coming when men will not tolerate wholesome teaching. They will want something to tickle their own fancies, and they will collect teachers who will pander to their own desires. They will no longer listen to the truth, but will wander off after man-made fictions.

For yourself, stand fast in all that you are doing, meeting whatever suffering this may involve. Go on steadily preaching the Gospel and carry out to the full the commission that God gave you.[19]

To explain imposes on the minister the duty of increasing the congregation's knowledge, by an attempt to make the people understand through the imparting of appropriate in-

[19] *The New Testament in Modern English,* translated by J. B. Phillips (New York: The Macmillan Company, 1958), p. 460.

formation. It widens, deepens, and heightens their grasp of the faith. But it does more than that; it enlarges their appreciation of the Good News. So we preach sermons on "Ecumenicity," "The Reason for Foreign Missions," "The Church as a Colony of the Kingdom of God," and "The Atonement," always remembering that those subjects have to be related to the Contemporary Situation if the explanation is to have relevance for daily living.

My wife has a very simple theory of preaching—from the point of view of the pew. She says, over and over again: "Speak to me as if I were intelligent but ignorant." Her desire is for more than an apprehension of the Word of God; she longs for comprehension, the comprehension which may result in appreciation.

The other general end which implements the *didactic* sermon goes beyond explanation; it is "to convince." This is the aim of the sermon which seeks to establish, to influence, to modify, or to change the beliefs of the congregation. It takes into account the intellectual attitudes—conservative and liberal, traditional and contemporary, fixed and tentative—of the listeners. It summons the minister and his people to mark, learn, and inwardly digest a new insight, a fresh interpretation, an unusual cause-effect relationship.

Preaching of this type carries me back to the first theological textbook which we studied in the Divinity Hall of Glasgow University—A. B. Bruce, *Apologetics; or, Christianity Defensively Stated.*[20] At the Duke Divinity School

[20] (New York: Charles Scribner's Sons, 1892.)

today Alan Richardson, *Christian Apologetics,* is a required textbook.[21]

An "apology" is a defense of the faith, and Christian classics of this type are scattered throughout the history of the church. Apologetics "is the study of the ways and means of defending Christian truth. . . . Apologetics deals with the relationship of the Christian faith to the wider sphere of man's 'secular' knowledge," says Richardson.[22] It is the preparatory work of a homiletical apologist, whose double task is both to defend the validity of the Good News for the believer, and to instruct him in a convincing counter-attack on the outlook of the non-Christian. For the best method of defense is sometimes an attack. But since preaching set in the context of worship is primarily, if not wholly, addressed to the believer, the sermon to convince is addressed to his obstinancies and blind spots and sub-Christian attitudes.

A sermon *to explain* the unexpectedly exciting debates of the Second Vatican Council and their implications for Protestantism may well be followed up by one *to convince* the congregation that what unites us with Rome is of more moment than that what separates us. A meditation *to revitalize* the congregation with the heavenly joy of Christmas may be succeeded during Christmastide by one on the meaning of the Incarnation (*to explain*) and by another on the reasons for belief in the Incarnation (*to convince*).

[21] (New York: Harper & Row, 1947.)
[22] *Ibid.,* p. 19.

Sermons during the latter half of the Sundays after Trinity —so well named "Kingdomtide" by the American Methodists—may move in the realm of Christian ethics, with a conscious effort to persuade the congregation to raise its spiritual sights in the area of man-to-man and group-to-group relations. The general end to convince is an effort for more comprehension, refined appreciation, and a deeper commitment.

There is one more general end—"to actuate." Here the minister desires "to obtain some definite observable performance." [23] He expects action—specific, seen, and soon. It may be to sing in the choir, or to teach in the Sunday school. It may be to give a second offering at the end of the service, or to sign a petition on the way out. It may be to work as a volunteer in a local hospital, or to take part in a parade. This general end, to actuate, depends on, at least, one of the others. One actuates through revitalizing, or through explaining, or through convincing. But it is wise to keep the primary general end, to actuate, uppermost and the others subordinate. (This is equally true if one is revitalizing through explaining.) *One general end may not be sufficient, but one should always be foremost.* Otherwise the sermon wobbles between two ends, or among three or four. It probably misses both or all. Let one dominate from introduction to conclusion.

"To actuate" does not expect a general or vague response. It is limited and explicit in its purpose. It knows what it

[23] Monroe, *Principles and Types of Speech*, p. 168.

wants—on Budget Sunday, or Every-Member-Canvass Sunday, or Rally Sunday. It has made plans for a follow-up. But it is salutary to know if the actuation is wise as well as precise. Before we preach a sermon whose end is to actuate, we would do well to recall the speech which Bob Zuppke, the American football coach, gave to his team in the field house at half time. The pep talk was packed with emotion and filled with incitement to action. It ended with these words, delivered in a thunderous tone: "Go out that door, through there to victory." But Zuppke pointed to the wrong door, and his boys, blinded by their tears, plunged through the door—into the swimming pool. He actuated, well but not wisely. But he did prove that the response to this general end is action—immediate and observable.

The sermon to actuate recovers the lost word in preaching—"How?" It brings the sermon down to earth, to an earth which is hard or dusty or muddy. It outlines how the Good News is incarnated, here and now. For the Word of God is always an applied truth.

So there are four general ends—to revitalize, to explain, to convince, to actuate. They will help us to aim our sermons at a particular target, at the pin instead of at the green. Each one will be chosen with the congregation in mind. But they are primarily for the minister's own concentration, as he decides the direction of the sermon while he sits at his study desk. They will help to protect him from purposelessness, for each offers him a compass point by which to steer the content of God's message and his.

III

Yet it is not always the preacher's fault that a sermon makes no dent on the listener. The pew is to be blamed as well as, if not as much as, the pulpit. Few of us outside the United States have to contend with this situation whimsically described in an American magazine:

It is safe to say that nobody who sat in the University of Kansas stadium during commencement exercises this month listened quite as intently as black-gowned Senior Lawrence Loftus. Graduate-to-be Loftus seemed almost entranced, in fact, by the words of McGruder E. Sadler, president of Texas Christian University, who spoke during the baccalaureate service. This solemn attentiveness moved some of the more restless to open curiosity; they noticed with a sense of shock that Loftus was wearing a hearing aid.

None had suspected that he was deaf, and they were startled to think that they were seeing a man who was caught up, not so much by the sentiments of a speech, but simply by the miracle of hearing fully for the first time. It was a moving moment—until a less sentimental colleague discovered that Loftus' earplug was actually connected with a pocket radio concealed beneath his gown. He was listening to the second game of a double-header between Kansas City and the Red Sox. The Red Sox won 4-3.[24]

Here is another incident more typical of both sides of the Atlantic. I was staying at a preparatory school in New

[24] "The Smuggler," reprinted from *Sports Illustrated*, June 27, 1955. Copyright 1955 Time Inc.

England, and I asked the headmaster's wife about the new minister in the village church. She replied that all was well, adding: "I particularly appreciate his preaching." I knew him for a worthwhile pastor, but I had never thought of him as an able preacher. I mentioned this. With a twinkle in her eye, she answered: "Oh, I never pay any attention to him. But he always preaches for thirty minutes, and in that half hour I can plan my week's work at the school. I never miss church."

It may be beyond the wit of man to grapple with this Kansas senior and this New England wife so that they listen to a sermon. Yet the final effectiveness of the sermon depends more on the hearing than on the preaching. In order to be doers of the Word, it is usually necessary, first of all, to be hearers of the Word. Recognizing the importance of the audience, Monroe goes a step beyond the four general ends. He narrows each specifically to the audience reaction. He asks the speaker to be sure, before he begins talking, of "the exact thing" he wants the listeners to feel, to understand, to believe, or to do by the time the address is concluded.[25] He insists that the desired response be specifically singled out before a word of the sermon is penned.

Therefore in addition to knowing his general end, the purposeful preacher knows also his specific intent, making sure that it is specific—narrowed and limited to a particular congregation on a given Sunday. The specific intent

[25] See Monroe, *Principles and Types of Speech,* pp. 172-76, 186-88.

avoids generalities; it individualizes. It remembers the refrain of Ellwood P. Dowd, the hero of the puckish play *Harvey*. When asked by a sympathetic friend: "Can I do anything for you?" Mr. Dowd's unvarying answer was: "Just what did you have in mind?" That is the unspoken question which the specific intent answers: "Just what did you have in mind, for this congregation, in this sermon?"

In the Duke Divinity School's courses in preaching, a student has to state his general end and his specific intent on the first page of his sermonic manuscript. The specific intent always begins with the same five words: "To help this congregation to. . . ." Then there follows a verb which is not synonomous with the verb in the general end but is complementary to it. The general end reveals the minister's purpose; the specific intent reveals the congregation's role in implementing that purpose. If he is preaching to revitalize the dormant faith in Easter, then the specific intent may well be: "To help this congregation to recall why confidence in the Resurrection message has always been at the heart of the life of the church, and still is." If he is preaching a sermon to explain what corporate worship is all about, then the specific intent may be: "To help this congregation to understand the order of worship used this morning in this service." If he is preaching on ecumenicity, to convince his people of its necessity and of its partial realization, his specific intent may be: "To help this congregation to believe that the ecumenical movement is the fragmented churches' reasoned understanding of the will of

God in our time, for our denomination." If his general end is to actuate for the purpose of an Every Member Canvass, his specific intent may be: "To help this congregation to give its services this afternoon in house-to-house visiting throughout the parish, with a view to offering a spiritual home to each nonchurchgoer." The specific intent develops, with particularity for the congregation, the less narrowed purpose of the general end.

Some years ago *Time* analyzed the forensic ability of John William Davis, the distinguished constitutional lawyer, who has argued more cases before the United States Supreme Court than any other lawyer, living or dead. It commented on his faculty for detecting the central issue in a case and for concentrating on that: "Other lawyers may try to put across a dozen ideas in a case. Davis prefers to narrow the issue to its lifeline: 'Always go for the jugular vein.' " [26]

It may not be wise to consider the pulpit as a courtroom, though many homileticians have made use of a legal analogy when they ask the minister to preach for a verdict. Moreover, going for the jugular vein may suggest homicide rather than soul saving. Yet there is wisdom in his analogy for us. We discover by investigation and interpretation what the lifeline of a passage of the Good News is. We decide which of the four general ends will help us to isolate and concentrate on it. Then through the specific intent we turn to application, so that the exegeted and expounded

[26] *Time*, December 21, 1953, p. 19.

aspect of the Good News may be related to a Contemporary Situation—and thus become a Word of God.

IV

The Reverend Dr. R. D. Whitehorn, Principal of Westminster College, Cambridge, once showed me a newspaper clipping about the discovery of an ancient holy ax in Ireland. There was one sentence in it which made us both chuckle and shudder: "The sacred character of the axe is conjectured from the absence of an effective cutting edge." Here is an unconscious, but valid, analysis of much of our preaching—it lacks an effective cutting edge. A blunt ax or a purposeless sermon has lost its virtue, its intended quality. A conscious knowledge of the general end and of the specific intent may sharpen the homiletical weapon. Or—to return to the paraphrased text in the introduction to this lecture—an intelligent use of the general ends and the specific intents will keep us from drawing a bow at a venture. We shall aim at Ahab or his cousins, his uncles, and his aunts. We may even hit more than one of them.

58479

CHAPTER V

the homiletical battery

Having looked together at the content of the Word of God, at its bifocal nature, at the need for exegesis and exposition and application, and at the general end and specific intent of the sermon, it ought to be obvious what the next step is. But we are not going to take it. Why? Because it is a veritable seven-league stride, much too long a step for a single lecture to take. It might well be the burden of an entire Warrack series. What is it? It is the matter of structuring the sermon, of organizing it for ordered delivery and aided remembrance. It is to everyone's advantage for the sermon to have a pattern, a controlled plan of development.

Lincoln Christian College

101

At Duke we had been working with eight different patterns for the structuring of a sermon. This year my young colleague, who has taken over the basic course in preaching, has added two more. To cover eight or ten different sermonic structures in one lecture would be to run a cross-country course at the speed of a hundred-yard dash. So, sorrowfully, but necessarily, we shall salute the patterns and pass by on the other side, except for one comment: Structuring is basic for the effective preaching of the Word. A competent pulpiteer—perhaps the most distinguished Episcopalian preacher in America—compares the pattern of a sermon to the "inflexible form of a sonnet":

The thing that makes the sonnet what it is is the fact that it says something important and that it says it in a particular way, the disciplined way of the sonnet. The secret, as it is in all art, is the perfect balance between significant content and effective form. While both are important, it is the purpose of this chapter to emphasize the fact that in preaching, as in all other creative work, without the form the content can be neither communicated nor remembered.[1]

With this deserving bow to the honorable reputation and compelling necessity of structure, let us move on to the matter of communication, that overworked but estimable word. Sermonic communication is the preaching and the hearing of the sermon in such a way that what is spoken and heard is understood by both the pulpit and the pew.

[1] Theodore Parker Ferris, *Go Tell the People* (New York: Charles Scribner's Sons, 1951), p. 53.

"Understood" is the key word of these lectures. In two of the Thirty-nine Articles of the Church of England, a phrase is used which has almost become the title of this Warrack series. It is "understanded of the people." In Article XXIV, the phrase refers to the language of public prayer: "It is a thing plainly repugnant to the Word of God, and the custom of the Primitive Church, to have public Prayer in the Church, or to minister the Sacraments, in a tongue not understanded of the people." The current Vatican Council has tentatively and hopefully recognized the truth of this Article, and we may now hear (or, hear of) the Mass being recited in the local vernacular. Article XXXV is closer to our immediate concern. It deals with the reading of the Homilies, which are to be spoken "diligently and distinctly, that they may be understanded of the people." The reading of other people's homilies is hardly the most apt description of our sermons, thought there is often more than a nodding acquaintance between the two. But our preaching is supposed to be in a tongue, in a vocabulary, in an idiom, in a thought form, in a homiletical language "understanded of the people." For a sermon, in the Reformed tradition, is not a sermon unless it is knowingly heard as well as wisely spoken.

While it is not semantically accurate to talk of the sermon as "dialogue" rather than "monologue," there is a basic truth in the use of "dialogue" for preaching. The minister speaks not only *to* his people and *for* his people, but *with* his people. He converses with them, listening to their unvoiced objections and questions, and trying to answer them as he moves through his address. He does not orate or monologize or soliloquize. He engages in a colloquy, a mutual discourse, even though he alone is speaking. Thus he has a chance of being "understanded of the people."

Let us look at this under the analogy of the pitcher and catcher in a baseball game. There would be more local color to the analogy if it could be developed in terms of the bowler and the wicket keeper in cricket. But the relationship of the pitcher and catcher is not quite the same as that of the bowler and wicket keeper. There is a unique intimacy between the two in baseball. Some of you despise baseball as a depraved form of rounders. I shall not comment on that misleading interpretation, except to say that I plan to stay with my baseball analogy. The pitcher and catcher together make up the "battery" in baseball. It is the theme of this lecture that the pitcher in the pulpit and the catcher in the pew together constitute the sermonic battery. Both are necessary. We shall look at each separately and then together.

I

The homiletical catcher is the person in the pew. He, including she, comes Sunday by Sunday to join in the worship of God. At one elongated point in the service he settles down to catch, or to ignore, what is pitched. The preacher, at a normal diet of worship, is working with believers, with people who are, by and large, within the community of faith, even though the membership is sometimes nominal and tenuous.

If the minister wishes to address nonbelievers, then he must find another field in which to play. Billy Graham shows his wisdom in choosing the secular auditorium, the football stadium, the exhibition hall, for his kerygmatic appeal to the uncoverted. So do the flying squads of "commandoes" who raid the public houses (saloons) for their audiences. The Salvation Army occupies the street corners. One church in Washington, D.C., has opened a coffee shop, away from the church premises, for its daily evening contacts with men and women of the world. Norman Maclean, when minister of St. Cuthbert's, Edinburgh, found the secular press his avenue for the broadcasting of the kerygma. This is so important, and unused, a medium that his journalistic experience is worth quoting. He had written a leading article at the request of the editor of *The Scotsman*; in his autobiography he comments on its reception:

That article was a revelation of the power of the Press. For letters poured in to the Editor. "I have had letters from ministers thanking us for it and saying that it had greatly assisted them," so wrote the Editor. A sermon on that subject would not bring even one letter! I then realised that the pulpit on the Bridges was much more influential than the pulpit below the Castle Rock—venerable and important though it was. And the reason is obvious. The pulpit in the *Scotsman* office reached several hundred thousand; that in church, a couple of thousand at most. And the reader was able to ponder the message, and read it several times if he did not grasp it at once, whereas the hearer was hurried from point to point and could not clarify by going back. The result was that I devoted more of my time and energy to the pulpit on the North Bridge than I previously had done and I continued for more than twenty years in all. It was a burdensome and additional labour to one already working hard, but it was worth while.[2]

There is a ministry to the unchurched. Some of us will specialize in it, at home and abroad.

But what about the churched? There they sit on the Lord's Day: young and old; male and female; married and single; widowed and divorced. Some are not interested. They hear and make no effort to understand; or they understand too well and, therefore, make no effort to hear. An old washerwoman said about her regular church going: "It's like this. It's not often I get such a comfortable seat, for so long a time, with so little to think about." This type of catcher is bored or resigned, present in body but absent in spirit, the despair of the young minister and the chronic discouragement of the old pastor. John Hutton, of Glasgow and *The British Weekly,* is said to have handled one such casual participant in drastic fashion. As a visiting preacher, he had just announced his text, when he noticed a parishioner settling down to sleep for the duration of the sermon. With focused eye, pointed finger, and peremptory voice, Hutton thundered: "Man, let us begin even—both

[2] Norman Maclean, *The Years of Fulfilment* (London: Hodder and Stoughton Ltd., 1953), p. 214.

awake. If you fall asleep *while* I am preaching, *you* win. If you stay awake, *I* win. But let us begin even." The galvanized congregation was enthralled. Their eyes swung back and forth between the aggressive preacher and the red-faced hearer. Hutton won; though it may be a matter of controversy if the Word was actually caught by anyone that day. This story is not told as a technique for producing insomnia in the pew. It is merely the recognition of one of the hard facts of homiletical life.

Other listeners accept the sermon almost as a Protestant form of the Sacrament of Penance. They know, theologically, that they are saved by grace, by the free grace of a God who loves extravagantly. But, psychologically, they are embarrassed by such undeserved generosity and feel that there ought to be a penalty, a satisfaction, a discipline of some sort to be accepted and endured. They are not unlike the naughty boy who said to his forgiving mother: "Don't forgive me! Thrash me! I always feel better after a thrashing." It may be unfair to compare the sermon to a thrashing, though the experience of the parish of Kilmany under the first eight years of Thomas Chalmers' preaching would suggest that such a metaphor is not entirely invalid.[3] I have some boyhood reminiscences of sermonic punishment, though it annoyed more than it stung. Is it because of the chastening, if not chastizing, effect of the sermon that an American judge recently "sentenced" an errant teen-ager to attend church for a year? Sydney Smith once described

[3] See F. W. Boreham, *A Bunch of Everlastings* (London: The Epworth Press, 1947), Chapter 1.

Scotland as "that knuckle-end of England—that land of Calvin, oat-cakes and sulphur," [4] but it was of English preaching that he wrote: "Preaching has become a bye-word for long and dull conversation of any kind; and who-ever wish to imply, in any piece of writing, the absence of everything agreeable and inviting, calls it a sermon." [5] This kind of sermon is tholed by the listeners.[6] They catch it. But do they catch it properly? Should it have been pitched for the purpose of penance? If the battery unitedly says "yes," it is going to make for a penal pulpit and a dour pew.

Still other hearers are puzzled by our preaching. At its best, they willingly acknowledge that it gives them daily guidance in personal contacts and in the intimate life of the family. That makes sense. Our Lord's ministry was to individuals, and his analogical sociology was dominated by the norm of the home, where God is a Father, and men and women are sons and daughters and siblings. But does the church have anything, either in theory or in fact, to say about the urgent, growing areas of impersonal relations: trade unions in conversation with employers' associations; old nations in disagreement with young nations? Moreover, are there areas of concord among the discordant but dog-matic opinions of the secular scientist and the philosopher of linguistic analysis and the non-Christian existentialist and the biblical expositor? Why do they differ so vehe-

[4] Lady Holland, *A Memoir of the Reverend Sydney Smith* (London: Longman, Brown, Green, and Longmans, 1855), I, 33.

[5] *Ibid.*, I, 81.

[6] "Thole" is a Scots word to "endure," "suffer." Robert Burns used it in "To a Mouse": "To thole the winter's sleety dribble."

mently? Does one merely change gear when he thinks as a scientist and when he reflects as a Christian, or does he change automobiles? Is the seeming discordance one of essence or one of language? Is all that is needed to make the Christian faith acceptable a current vocabulary?

These are the questions of good folk, good but puzzled. They give themselves to corporate worship—they praise, they pray, they listen with concentrated attention to the reading and the preaching of the Word. They will catch almost anything thrown at them. But they sometimes wish something else were pitched, something pertinent to their conflicting loyalties.[7] They wish the game made more sense. They wish there was something which unified them as sons and husbands and fathers and workers and voters, or as daughters and wives and mothers and workers and voters. They know, they think, they hope that religion has the answer. So they come to church, and they listen. They do not always agree with the Word preached. But they keep coming.

Then there are the faithful, the pillars of the kirk, the God-fearers, the devout. They hear and are blessed. They act in their blessedness; and others are blessed, and are converted, and come to hear. There are some churches which are still filled to overflowing once, twice, three times on the Lord's Day. Is it not because the pitcher and catcher understand each other, trust each other, work with each other, encourage each other? The catcher is a key figure; the

[7] See A. D. Lindsay, *The Two Moralities: Our Duty to God and to Society* (London: Eyre and Spottiswoode, 1940).

game cannot go on without him. Moreover, if he misses the ball, the fault may be his. In baseball such a missed ball is scored against him. It goes down in the records as a "passed ball," and the catcher is charged with an error. Yes, sometimes, the pew is to be blamed for the sermon when communication failed and no results were produced.

II

In the game of baseball there is another way of scoring the ball which goes sailing past the catcher. It may be a "wild pitch." Then it is noted as an error against the pitcher. No catcher could be reasonably expected to handle such a delivery. So let us look at the other half of the battery— the pitcher in the pulpit, the preacher. What will make him the kind of preacher who will be heard, understood, and interpreted in the daily ongoing life of the congregation?

There are two necessary qualities of the pitcher which time allows us to assume, to state, and to leave quickly. First, he is sure of his commitment. He is God's man, and he knows the God whose man he is. When Francis Bacon spoke in the House of Commons, the benches were crowded and quiet. He himself tells us the primary reason for this absorbed interest in what he had to say: "I have spoke out of the fountain of my heart." [8] He spoke from feeling depths, from first-hand knowledge, and from com-

[8] Bowen, *Francis Bacon: The Temper of a Man*, p. 113.

mitment. So should the minister. There are two lines from the drama of Job which might well be every minister's *confessio fidei:*

> I had heard of thee by hearsay,
>   but now mine eyes have seen thee (42:5, Moffatt).

He knows the God whose man he is.

To this quality of commitment is added that of preparation. We have talked about some aspects of this preparation in the previous lectures: a growing knowledge of the content of the Good News; an increasing awareness of its essential and intimate relation with a Contemporary Situation; the almost daily deskwork of a scribe trained for the kingdom of heaven; the detailed understanding of the particular purpose of each sermon. This is hard, disciplined, time-consuming work. We have all heard the ideal and terrifying slogan: "One hour of preparation for each minute of delivery." The minister in the pulpit is a prepared man.

Granted commitment and preparation as the *sine qua non* of the preacher, what other qualities will enable him to work effectively with his catcher? There is an awareness of his identification with his congregation. When I was a student assistant, my mother taught me that fact of ecclesiastical life in a simple and memorable way. I wrote out every word of my sermons—I still do—and gave them to her for criticism and emendation. The one correction which has stayed with me is that, wherever possible, mother changed the pronoun "you" to "we" or "us." Now and again, she would allow "you and I." A catcher was telling a pitcher that a sermon is a united effort, a joint piece of work, a constant partnership, a mutual participation.

There are various ways in which one may implement this sense of unity and community. One is pastoral visitation, a first-hand encounter with one's members in their homes, in their business (at appropriate times), in their avocations. Have we ever gone with the beadle to a football match? He can give us casual, but wise, hints on the folk who come to the kirk or who stay away. So can policemen and taxicab drivers and doctors. So can the office bearers, and the Sunday school teachers, and the organist—sometimes!

Another way is to visualize the members as we sit in our studies wording the sermon. What about the man who always comes alone, because his wife is a Roman Catholic and because his children care nothing about public worship? What about the nurse who regularly turns up in uniform, because she is going on duty immediately after the service? What about the officer in the armed forces, a spiritual descendant of the Roman centurion who loved the Jewish nation to the extent of building a synagogue? What about the woman in the unusual hat, who is so worried about life after death? What about that office stenographer whose days on earth are numbered, and who knows it? There they sit, or stand, looking at us across the study desk, each silently asking: "Will you keep me in mind when you write your sermons, for they are *our* sermons?"

Pastoral visiting and later visualization are two ways for us to know our catchers, for us to know them as more than people in general. When we know them as individuals, we come to love them as persons. Someone asked Abraham Lincoln if he liked a certain person. He answered: "No." A second question followed: "Do you know him?" Lincoln's answer was instant: "Of course I don't know him. If I knew him, I would like him." My heart is not as large as Lincoln's. I may not be able to like everyone whom I know. But, as a Christian, I am under orders to love them, to have goodwill toward them. Such commanded, disciplined love may develop into "kindly affection" (Rom. 12:10). Then I may very well like them, too! Such love and affection can work wonders for the preacher and his hearers. One zealous preacher in the States was dismissed by his congregation because Sunday after Sunday he shook them over the mouth of hell, until their hair was singed and their nostrils choked with the fumes of brimstone. Another minister took his place. He also majored in hellfire. Yet the congregation accepted him with joy, and listened to him with profit. In what way did the two preachers differ? A listener answered the question quite simply: "Sure, this second man preaches hell, too. But it pains him to do so." He spoke about hell in love. He had compassion. I do not know for a fact, but I surmise that he used the pronoun "we." He identified himself with his people. He was accepted.

If there were time, I would spend the rest of this lecture

on style, on conversational style. The day of flamboyant oratory, of imperial exhortation, has not entirely passed from the pulpit. But more and more preachers are adopting a conversational approach to delivery, in vocabulary, in sentence structure, and in utterance. The public address system is making this possible even in large churches which are acoustical mausoleums. Style is the bridge between the pulpit and the pew. Across it march the prepared thoughts of a committed man to a congregation which is ready to listen, or may be helped to listen, if certain qualities of conversational style be kept in mind. The preacher who had better keep them in mind is the one who takes a full manuscript into the pulpit.

Conversational style is oral rather than literary. It is written to be spoken, not to be read. For this reason a spoken sermon probably reads badly, unless the reader can visualize and rehear the speaker. The sentences are short, almost staccato. There are many principal clauses and few relative clauses. The vocabulary is simple. Key terms are defined and the definitions are repeated. Repetition is essential, for the congregation cannot go back and reread what has been said. The minister does this for them by regular, clarifying repetition. Since good conversation is at least dialogue, the use of the rhetorical question is a valid device to catch the attention of the listener. It brings him into a conscious participation with the developing thought: "What would you have said to Jesus when he asked his disciples: 'Will you also desert me?' " Such a query lassoes the listener.

Conversational style is picturesque. It paints a picture. As the old Arabian proverb has it: It turns the ear into an eye. It may turn the ear into any of the senses. Here is a secular example of picturesque style which the dean emeritus of the Duke Medical School brought to my attention:

There is in England and some other British countries a tradition of good writing and a tradition of much good reading that improves writing. Let me read to you, as an extreme example, a letter to his employer written by a day laborer—a bricklayer—in the Barbados and reproduced in a recent *Manchester Guardian,* which has some of the distinctive, pleasing qualities of the best English writing: clarity, simplicity, an archaic flavor, and dramatic effect dependent on understatement. Here is the letter:

> "Respected Sir:
>   When I got to the building, I found that the hurricane had knocked some bricks off the top. So I rigged up a beam with a pulley at the top of the building and hoisted up a couple of barrels full of bricks. When I had fixed the building, there was a lot of brick left over.
>   I hoisted the barrel back up again and secured the line at the bottom, and then went up and filled the barrel with extra bricks. Then I went to the bottom and cast off the line.
>   Unfortunately, the barrel of bricks was heavier than I was and before I knew what was happening the barrel started down, jerking me off the ground. I decided to hang on and halfway up I met the barrel coming down and received a severe blow on the shoulder.

> I then continued to the top, banging my head against the beam and getting my finger jammed in the pulley. When the barrel hit the ground it bursted its bottom, allowing all the bricks to spill out.
>
> I was heavier than the empty barrel and so started down again at high speed. Halfway down, I met the barrel coming up and received severe injuries to my shins. When I hit the ground, I landed on the bricks, getting several painful cuts from the sharp edges.
>
> At this point I must have lost my presence of mind, because I let go of the line. The barrel then came down giving me another heavy blow on the head and putting me in the hospital."

All that our bricklayer friend wanted was some workmen's compensation. If British justice is as justly famed as British composition, I am sure that he obtained it.[9]

Not many of us have the knack of such clear, picturesque, dramatic storytelling. But it is not to be despised, not even in preaching the Word of God. Was style one reason why the common people heard Jesus gladly? They said of him that he didn't speak like the average minister (Matt. 7:29). Did his style have nothing to do with his authority?

Such simplicity must not be confused with vacuity or fatuity. There are technical terms, old and new, which have a rightful place in the sermon: grace, faith, atonement, Holy Ghost; even salvation history, eschatology, and agape. John Baillie told of a newspaper reporter confronting him

[9] Charles Hitch, "Reflections on Oxford and Education," *The American Oxonian*, XLVI (January, 1959), 7-8.

at the Evanston Conference of the World Council of Churches and asking this question about agape: "What is this 'a-g-a-p-e' you all talk about? I looked it up in the dictionary and it means 'with the mouth open.'" We are living in an age of "gobbledegook," "bafflegab," "officialeese," with its abandonment of simplicity, its pseudolearned vocabulary, its capacity to abuse, to mutilate, even to murder, the king's English. The aforementioned dean emeritus of our Medical School provided me with an example of this kind of writing which should be a warning to us in our particular bailiwick:

Some letter writers appear to agree with the oft-quoted statement of Samuel Johnson that "words were invented to conceal thought."

As an example, let's review the experience of the plumber who wrote to the National Bureau of Standards. He said he found that hydrochloric acid opens plugged pipes quickly, and asked whether it was a good thing for a plumber to use.

A scientist at the Bureau replied as follows:

"The uncertain reactive processes of hydrochloric acid place pipe in jeopardy when alkalinity is involved. The efficiency of the solution is indisputable, but the corrosive residue is incompatible with metallic permanence."

The plumber wrote back, thanking the Bureau for telling him that this method was all right. The scientist was disturbed about the misunderstanding, and showed the correspondence to his boss—another scientist—who immediately wrote the plumber:

"Hydrochloric acid generates a toxic and noxious residue

which will produce submuriate invalidating reactions. Consequently, some alternative procedure is preferable."

The plumber wrote back and said he agreed with the Bureau —hydrochloric acid works just fine. Greatly disturbed, the two scientists took their problem to the top boss. The next day the plumber received this telegram:

"Don't use hydrochloric acid. It eats hell out of the pipes." [10]

As G. K. Chesterton once remarked: "The language is theological, though it has no doctrinal import." But the correspondence carries import for us who preach. If our general end is "to explain" or "to convince," it is advisable to use words which, by their own clarity, or by careful definition in understandable language, do explain or may convince.

Since most of our people are Jewish rather than Greek in their understanding of the faith, they prefer a picturesque and practical elucidation of the Good News to an abstract analysis and synthesis, however true. Therefore, it is the wise minister who uses illustrative material to clarify his proposition and subpropositions. There are three criteria to keep in mind about illustrations. First, are they valid? Do they have an essential relationship with the subject matter? An illustration about "faith" does not necessarily throw light on the meaning of "hope." Second, are they pertinent? Does the congregation understand them? Do they fall easily within their ken? You may say that I failed this test by making use of a baseball analogy (in

[10] Margaret Case Harriman, *And the Price is Right* (Cleveland: The World Publishing Company, 1958), pp. 264-65.

Scotland!) to throw light on the joint responsibility of pulpit and pew for the sermon. *Touché*. Third, are they varied? Do they reach differing age groups, both sexes, various interests? Moreover, do they reach them *from* and *in* today's life? That wee boy in Holland who has been holding his finger in a crack in the dyke is a pensioner by now and ought to be honorably retired, certainly from homiletical duty outside the Netherlands. Illustrations are necessary in most sermons; they are almost indispensable where the general end is "to revitalize" or "to actuate."

All of us know the famous definition of a sermon as "truth through personality," the reincarnation of the Good News. But there is a better definition. A sermon is the truth, plus the man, plus style. The truth comes to life for the congregation where the committed and prepared preacher, *en rapport* with his people, makes use of a mastered oral style to transmit the Word of God. From long years of teaching, I have come to the conclusion that the difference between a B and an A student is seldom a knowledge of facts, or ideas, or principles. The difference is usually in the way in which each makes use of words to express the equally known data. This is also true of preaching. The pitcher must throw the kind of delivery, which he has mastered, in such a way that the catcher can handle it.

III

We have thought of the combined efforts of the pew and the pulpit by looking at each separately, though always aware of the relation of each to the other. Now let us look at them together, working as a battery. The simplest way to do this is to state a proposition and then to illustrate it with valid, pertinent, and varied case studies. Here is the proposition: The sermon is the joint production of the clergy and the laity working consciously together. The members of the ruling body—the Kirk Session, the Board of Stewards, the Vestry—the Sunday school teachers, the Parish visitors, the heads of organizations are responsible, with the minister, for the preaching and hearing of the Word. It is not a job for a solitary worker, a lone wolf, a male prima donna, but for a team. A sermon is the combined effort of cleric and layman, the mutual enterprise of the beloved community, the harmonious battery of pulpit and pew. Is such a proposition true, anywhere in the ecclesiastical world?

There is an Episcopalian church where a representative group of the congregation gathers with the minister after (or before) Morning Prayer to discuss *next* Sunday's sermon with him. Inasmuch as they follow the Christian Year, they concentrate on the Collect, the Epistle, and the Gospel for the succeeding Sunday in *The Book of Common Prayer*. They have done their homework by reading the "propers" ahead of time, and they can ask intelligent lay questions about the three sections, suggest subjects for analysis, confess their problems in implementing the faith. The minister picks it up from there.

Several churches in America, and at least one in Scotland, are making use of the dialogue sermon, with two partici-

pants conjointly expounding the Word. Sometimes one
asks questions and the other answers. Sometimes they take
turns in questioning and answering each other. As a rule
the two speakers are clergy, but they deal with topics suggested by the members. There is no reason why a layman
should not be one of the participants. I can think of one
devout doctor in Durham, North Carolina, who could en-
lighten most of us on *agathanasia*: the right of the patient
to make a good death, the right of any man to die with
dignity. He rightly and soundly distinguishes between
agathanasia and euthanasia.[11] The Cathedral of St. John
the Divine in New York City developed three-cornered
conversations at Sunday Evensong back in the summer of
1954; a longer series was broadcast on Sundays in July
and August of that year. The subject was the seven deadly
sins. A layman took the role of the tempted soul; one clergyman was the tempter; another was the voice of the church.
No one won. But there was the recurring stimulus for
those watching or listening to look into their own souls and
to continue the debate there. The style was lively and col-
loquial, with frequent flashes of wit.[12]

At the Preaching Clinic for twenty clergymen, held for
two weeks each summer under the auspices of the Duke
Divinity School, a recurring feature, one evening each
year, has been "laymen's night." To hear the catchers'

[11] Thomas T. Jones, M. D., "Dignity in Death: The Application
and Withholding of Interventive Measures," *The Journal of the
Louisiana State Medical Society*, CXIII (1961), 180-83.
[12] James A. Pike and Howard A. Johnson, *Man in the Middle*
(Greenwich: The Seabury Press, 1956).

reaction to preaching is both devastating and salutary for the pitchers. One housewife, shyly but determinedly, discussed delivery. She was very willing as a sinful Christian to be ashamed or embarrassed or wooed into a closer walk with God. But she would not be yelled at. She could not understand why the Good News of the Kingdom should be shouted, or declaimed, or bellowed. She could not imagine her Lord roaring the Sermon on the Mount. She believed that when he opposed a point of view, his anger was penetrated with sorrow and love. A fellow layman, a historian and a dean, discussed faulty enunciation, failure to be careful in the choice of the exact word needed, incorrect grammar, poor sentence structure, wobbly organization. It was a hushed group of pitchers who heard these catchers talk. Of course, the clerical audience tried to wiggle out of the dilemma by pointing out that the man in the pew should come for more than the sermon. But the lay folk, who were nothing if not logical, pointed out that this was a clinic in *preaching,* and they had been asked to discuss the sermon. With a gleam in his eye, softened by a twinkle, the Dean asked if they would like to hear his comments on the music and the prayers. The clergy, wisely and chastenedly, said "No!" Yet the clergy voted that such an evening be repeated each year. This year's clinic is going a step further. The local town congregations are being asked to supply critics at the practice-preaching sessions, so that each preacher may receive lay as well as clerical reaction to his sermon. This is going to be a summer school of training for the homiletical batteries.

In the February issue of *The Pulpit*, there is an account of an experiment made in a Texas pulpit.[18] The rector was discussing the reaction to a memorial notice carried in the previous week's church bulletin. It ran as follows:

IN MEMORIAM

Killed while worshiping God in Birmingham,
Sunday, September 15, 1963

Carol Robertson   Cynthia Wesley

Addie Mae Collins   Denise McNair

May Almighty God be merciful unto us
and grant them eternal rest.

These four Negro children were the victims of malignant racism. No one objected to the remembrance of them, but some parishioners wondered why there was not also a memorial to two white women who had been killed in Houston the previous week by a Negro man. What the rector said in comparing and contrasting the two incidents is not immediately relevant for us. But the ending of his sermon is. Here are the last two paragraphs:

I pray your love and understanding as together we try in all that we do to be faithful to the God who loves all men in the world enough to give up his Son on the cross that together we might have the victory.

[18] G. H. Jack Woodard, "Some Important Differences." Copyright 1964 Christian Century Foundation. Reprinted by permission from *The Pulpit*, Vol. XXXV, No. 2 (February, 1964).

Usually you have no real opportunity to reply to my sermons, but this time you do. The ushers will now pass out a questionnaire which will give you a chance to let me know what you think. Please do not sign it unless you want to, and if for any reason you should not want to fill one out, then I suggest you join me in silent prayer for the next five minutes while those who do want to reply work on their paper. Just leave the questionnaires in the pews when you leave the church, and I will appreciate it.

There were four questions on the questionnaire, and 65 per cent of the adults present at the two morning services answered these questions:

1. I (agree) (disagree) with the substance of today's sermon.
2. I (would like) (do not need) to have Mr. Woodard come by and discuss it with me.
3. In my opinion our parish and diocese (is doing enough) (is not doing enough) (is doing too much) work for racial understanding and justice.
4. I want my senators and congressman to vote:
    a. (For) (Against) the civil rights bill with the exception of the section on public accommodations.
    b. (For) (Against) the public accommodations section of the civil rights bill.

The majority was with the rector. Thirty-five percent wanted him to come by and discuss the sermon with them. Seventy-four present believed that the parish was not doing enough for racial understanding and justice. This experiment was a conscious effort to link the spoken Word and the response.

There is one more case study, one which came directly to my attention when I was an official sermon critic at the Preaching Clinic at Union Theological Seminary in Richmond, Virginia. A young Congregational minister had chosen as his theme one which he had already preached to his own people on "The Christian Attitude to Mercy Killing." He was in favor of euthanasia and—with a reasonable proposition, with valid and pertinent illustrations—he developed the subject by juxtaposing "Thou shalt not kill" and "Blessed are the merciful." There was nothing brash or smart about his presentation. It was offered to us with care, with understanding, and with vast sympathy. That sermon was heard. A dropped pin would have been a thunderclap in the preaching room. The ensuing criticism was vigorous, multifarious, and sympathetic. When the formal discussion was over, I asked him how he managed to tackle such a controversial theme with such irenic results. There were, of course, personal dedication and sound preparation. But here is the unique plus. Thirty minutes before the service begins, all the deacons in his church gather in the vestry to pray with, and for, the minister. At five minutes to the hour all but one escort him to the pulpit in full view of the congregation, and then move to join their own families. The deacon who remains in the vestry continues in intercessory prayer for the minister throughout the entire service. The young preacher added: "If they and I had known at what hour I was to preach this sermon here for criticism, one of my deacons would have been in the vestry at home, up North." No wonder he preaches well. No wonder he can safely tackle difficult subjects. No wonder his hearers can catch the sermons. Through the office bearers they have let him know that the expounded Word is their responsibility too. Cooperative listening surely accompanies corporate prayer. That must be a blessed church. It, too, has made of preaching a mutual enterprise. There the homiletical battery is effectively at work.

IV

The sermon, then, is not the minister's task alone. For communication is possible only when pulpit and pew are aware that each depends on the other—consciously, cooperatively, continually. Preaching, like the rest of worship, is a joint production of clergy and laity "for the glory of the Creator and the relief of man's estate," to use an expression of Francis Bacon. The church, under God, depends on the close, and ever closer, harmony of the pulpit and the pew, where the congregation is "understanded" of the minister, and the preacher is "understanded of the people."

251
C625

58479